Walter Barlow Stevens

Through Texas

a series of interesting letters

Walter Barlow Stevens

Through Texas
a series of interesting letters

ISBN/EAN: 9783744744591

Printed in Europe, USA, Canada, Australia, Japan

Cover: Foto ©Andreas Hilbeck / pixelio.de

More available books at **www.hansebooks.com**

THROUGH TEXAS.

A SERIES OF

INTERESTING LETTERS

By WALTER B. STEVENS,

SPECIAL CORRESPONDENT OF THE

ST. LOUIS GLOBE-DEMOCRAT.

ILLUSTRATED.

1892.

INTRODUCTION.

The following letters appeared in the *St. Louis Globe-Democrat* during the fall of 1892. Mr. Walter B. Stevens, the *Globe's* special correspondent, is one of the most acute observers and interesting writers on western life and progress, and this series of interesting letters, "Through Texas," has attracted widespread attention, and has been read with pleasure and profit by thousands. They present a graphic picture of Texas, its social and industrial life blended into charming narrative.

There is no exaggeration of the State's resources; the letters were not written to boom Texas; only for the information of a large and interested circle of readers. However, they may be made to answer a double purpose, and those contemplating a change of location, or desiring to settle in a new and growing country, will find the facts on the resources of Texas, with which they are filled, of great value.

With this object in view, the General Passenger Department of the Missouri Pacific Railway and Iron Mountain Route has had them compiled and printed in this convenient form for distribution, in order to meet the wide demand for them from all parts of the country. Their reliability renders them indispensable to the home-seekers, and makes them a valuable hand-book on Texas for some time to come.

Additional copies can be obtained from the company's agents, or by addressing

H. C. TOWNSEND,

General Passenger and Ticket Agent, ST. LOUIS, MO.

THROUGH TEXAS.

A SERIES OF INTERESTING LETTERS

FROM THE SPECIAL CORRESPONDENT OF THE

ST. LOUIS GLOBE-DEMOCRAT.

THROUGH TEXAS.

A Story of Development from $4 an Acre to $400,000 a Ranch.

The Profits of Horse Breeding—A Bunch of Galloways—Coach and Percheron—Cyclone Cellar Building—The Funniest Thing in the State.

Special Correspondence of the Globe-Democrat.

SANBORN RANCH, TEXAS, July 23.—Henry B. Sanborn, a New Yorker, came to Texas in 1875 to introduce a certain manufacture of barbed wire. Not long after his arrival he bought a piece of land in Grayson County. The price was $4 an acre. Later on Mr. Sanborn bought other pieces. He fenced them and put on stock. All of this time he was carrying on his wire agency and attending to his regular business at Houston, hundreds of miles south. The ranch was his recreation. It grew until in one compact body there were 10,300 acres. Selecting the branches of breeding which interested him most, Mr. Sanborn gradually improved his stock until his coach and draft horses and his thoroughbred bulls were known to all Texas. This Sanborn ranch, developed from a small beginning in the way described, has just passed into the possession of a stock company. The accepted valuation put upon the property is $400,000. This is $25 an acre, or $260,000 for the land and $140,000 for the stock. The purchasers are Shannon C. Douglass, Judge Charles L. Dobson and other Missourians. Mr. Sanborn retains an interest and agrees to give the ranch his personal attention for the present.

A ranch of 10,300 acres must be traversed to be appreciated. A man on a mowing machine stopped when he came to the end of the half-mile swath to tell the way to the Sanborn place.

"This, said he, "is part of it where we're cutting and baling hay. You struck the ranch about a half mile back. If you want to go to the house, keep right on down the road till you come to a lane on the left. That is about three-quarters of a mile. Turn up the lane and go till you come to a gate on the right. That's about half a mile. Turn in at the gate and follow the road. You'll come to the house in about a mile." Half an hour afterward the team, by brisk driving and by persistent refusals to let the young driver try his Winchester on all of the turtle doves sitting on telegraph wires, pulled up beside the big white house from the broad porch of which Mr. Sanborn was monarch of all he surveyed until last week he signed the title deeds. It took nearly an hour of good driving to reach the house after the eastern boundary was passed. And the house and outlying farms and stables are about half way on an east and west line across the ranch. Mr. Sanborn can sit on his porch and see the cars cross his line so far away they look like toys. He can see them grow larger until they stop at Sanborn station on his own land. He can follow the long trail of smoke for ten or fifteen minutes before the other boundary is crossed. Then he can go to his back door and just distinguish his own cattle

A $400,000 RANCH.

THE GALLOWAYS.

looking about as large as ants three and four miles away in the direction opposite from the railroad. That is what a 10,000-acre ranch means.

The books of the Sanborn ranch have just been summarized for the benefit of the new company. With the figures before him, Mr. Sanborn frankly gave an insight into the business. "The books," said he, "show that the sales of stock for the year ending with the 1st of this month amounted to $40,595.65. The sales for the year ending July 1, 1891, were $33,470.42; for the year ending July 1, 1890, they were $23,302.96, and for the year ending July 1, 1889, they were $34,308.26."

"What does the other side of the balance sheet show, Mr. Sanborn?"

"The expenses of operating this place have run from $12,000 to $15,000 a year."

"How many men do you employ?"

"From eight to fifteen."

The men, Mr. Sanborn explained, were employed chiefly in taking care of the stock. A considerable quantity of hay is cut. On the whole ranch the tilled land is only about 300 acres. This land is rented to farmers on shares, one-third of the crop being taken for rental.

"That rented ground, taking one year with another," Mr. Sanborn said, "has paid 10 per cent and over on a valuation of $25 an acre."

Last year his share of the crop on this rented land yielded him about $4 an acre. At a time when there is so much talk about "per capita," farm mortgages, corn burning and that range of themes, the figures from Mr. Sanborn's books are very interesting.

In the way of "cow stock," the pride of the Sanborn ranch is a herd of pure bred Galloways. Short legged, long haired, black as the waxy soil after a wetting, hornless, shaggy-headed, the Galloways make a striking picture on the pasture scape when the grass is turning brown. They feed close together and they keep moving. Their restless energy is one thing that strongly commends them here. The Texas cattlemen want a brute that will rustle for its living when the grass is short and the northers come.

"The Shorthorn," Supt. Shero said, "will get discouraged when the season is bad. He must be helped out with a little feed. The Hereford will hump up and lose flesh when the cold strikes him. But the Galloway will keep going and hunting something to eat. After a hard season the weaker of these herds will get down in the mud sometimes, and won't have ambition enough to get up again without help. You never see a Galloway get in that fix; he is always able to take care of himself. That is one of the big points in his favor for Texas."

On the Sanborn ranch black cattle are not raised for beef. The strain is too fine and expensive. Thoroughbred Galloways are grown and sold to head the herds of Shorthorn and Herefords on other ranches. The cross gives the breed which finds its way into market. It produces an animal with finer hair, longer legs and greater weight than the Galloway, but the strength of the strain shows itself in the black hide and the hornless head.

The short legs and big bodies make the Galloway the most deceptive looking of "cow brutes." On the Sanborn place it is very easy to get a bet on the weight of a given Galloway, and it is easier to lose it. Once upon a time Dr. Grant, of Sherman, a man with a fund of information on Texas horses and Texas cattle, encountered the deception. He had a dispute with Mr. Sanborn about the weight of a young Galloway they had been looking at.

"I'll bet you a hat you can't guess the weight of that brute within 300 pounds," said Mr. Sanborn.

The Doctor smiled sarcastically, looked the Galloway up and down and from end to end. "Six hundred pounds," he said.

That evening the bet came up for further discussion at the house.

THE IMPORTED PERCHERON.

Supt. Shero, when he heard of it, said to the Doctor: "I'd like to bet a hat that is a bad bet, Doctor."

Dr. Grant tapped his thinker, and with increased sarcasm said: "This head might be found in a Penitentiary, but never in an asylum."

The boys were told to cut out the particular Galloway, and get him on the scales. He weighed 1130 pounds. Dr. Grant looked at the indicator and then at the brute. "I wouldn't have believed there could have been so much meat in that much hide," he said.

When the artist caught the Galloways for the illustration they were bunched together so closely that their sides rubbed. The bunch was making the double motion of the funnel-shaped cloud. The individual brutes were moving round and round in a close circle, and the bunch itself was drifting slowly along the wire fence, all grazing.

"You'll have to get 'em quick," said Mr. Shero from his horse, "or they'll be off," and

FORGERON.

so the drifting and at the same time revolving bunch was caught on the double movement, with heads and bodies and tails all mixed up. "That is the way those brutes feed, close together, just as you see 'em," Mr. Shero explained. There is no other cow native on the broad Texas prairies quite like the Galloway. The Polled Angus are somewhat like the Galloways in appearance. They are black and hornless, but they have longer legs, finer hair and more range of body. That is where the Durham blood comes in. Mr. Sanborn says the Polled Angus is a breed made originally by crossing the Galloway and the Durham.

The raising of Galloways is only a side issue. It is as a horse ranch that the Sanborn place has made its fame. Mr. Sanborn has tried several experiments. He indulged in thoroughbreds for a short time, but discarded them. This Texas climate puts fire into a naturally sluggish strain. It makes of thoroughbreds an animal which is a holy terror in horse flesh, spirited and excitable almost beyond training. With trotting stock better results have been obtained. "It is as natural," said Mr. Sanborn, with a laugh, "for a horse raiser to drift into trotting stock as it is for a cotton dealer to get in the way of selling futures, or for a grain buyer to add option trading to his business." And so Mr. Sanborn has drifted into the breeding of trotters to the extent of having a $25,000 stallion, Prinmont, at the head of a stable and a lot of youngsters which show better than 2:40 without training. But the breeding of trotters is not the legitimate field of the ranch. Coach and draft horses are the two branches to which the most of the land, the most of the attention is devoted. The barns and stables hold the sires of the scores of colts which beside their dams make interesting pasture scenes.

"This seems to be the natural home of the horse," Mr. Sanborn said. "Horses can stand in Texas what would kill them North. We ride and drive and work horses in this region in a way that would be impossible elsewhere. The climate develops the lung power and staying qualities."

This remark was fairly well illustrated a few minutes later. Supt. Shero and one of his assistants rode into a big pasture and proceeded to round up a bunch of mares with their coach strain progeny for inspection. A 2-months colt in Texas is wilder than an In-

A TEXAS CYCLONE CELLAR.

dian. Apparently some of the youngsters took the visit of the superintendent as the suggestion for a frolic. With heads and tails up the colts started and the dams followed with maternal devotion. The sun was blazing down from right overhead. The mercury was away up in the nineties. Across the pasture, a mile wide, up and down and round and round went mares and colts, superintendent and assistant in a mad chase. When, in about fifteen minutes, the drove was corraled where two wire fences angled, there was some puffing, a good deal of perspiration, a lost hat, but no suffering. The superintendent treated the chase as quite an every-day affair. A little later mares were grazing and colts were nipping and kicking at each other as if nothing had happened to make them tired.

The head of Forgeron looks out of his stable window in the initial of the date line of this letter. He is a black French coach stallion, with a pedigree a great deal longer than those which qualify Sons of the American Revolution. Forgeron comes from the home of his ancestors—France—but he has been in Texas long enough to be naturalized. It is one of the inconsistencies of this natural horse-breeding climate of North Texas that the horses raised here can stand anything, but the horses brought here from the North have to undergo a more or less critical period of change before they become adapted to the conditions here. This lesson of acclimating is what the horse and cattle raisers of Texas paid a big price to learn. The time came when they wanted something better than ponies and long-horns. They did as they usually do in everything. They plunged on fine stock. They bought from the breeders up North fine horses by the car-load, and fine bulls by the train-load. They unloaded them in Texas and turned them loose, only to add large items to loss account at end of the year. It was one of many costly experiments which have taught Texas wisdom. After that Texas breeders adopted a different policy. They brought few and the very choicest of animals, some from the North, some from foreign countries. They housed and cared for these importations carefully. On this basis they built up their own breeding establishments. No Texan now goes North for stallions or bulls except for high-priced individuals with which to infuse new blood on his own breeding ranch. The system has undergone entire change.

The Percherons are the emphatic features of the Sanborn place. They are strong in numbers, strong in weight and strong in every way. There is, it seems, a good, profitable demand for good draft horses.

"Don t you find this general application of electricity to street cars is cutting down the demand for horses and reducing the prices?"

Mr. Sanborn shook his head and replied: "No; we have seen no effect on the demand for horses from the use of electricity. The horses we breed are taken for express business, fire departments and heavy work. But, speaking generally, I don't think that horse-raising will be affected seriously by the use of electricity for motive power. If they use electricity for cars, they must have horses to haul the coal to the power house. Where horse power is dispensed with in one place it is called into service in others. The country needs more and more horses."

THE JENNETS AND THEIR YOUNG.

Now and then, in Texas, there can still be seen a brand which marks the whole flank or shoulder of a horse. Some of these hieroglyphics look as if they had been made with a butcher knife while the animal was struggling for liberty. Slashes 18 inches long, with ridges of hair only partially hiding the scar, tell how things were done at one time. On the Sanborn ranch the branding is reduced to the briefest possible record. It is also made a part of the pedigree system. To find names for colts coming by the hundreds every year would be too great a tax on ingenuity. The youngsters are numbered as they come. The numbers, in as small figures as can be distinguished, are branded upon the shoulder. The colts are recorded by the same numbers in the pedigree book. Among so many it is impossible to distinguish in the usual way, by colors and marks. And so the entry is limited to "Colt, No. blank; dam, No. blank." This is brevity. The brand on the shoulder identifies the colt with the corresponding number in the record book. The number of the dam affords the means of tracing back the pedigree on that side. It is all very simple. "No. 1076, got by 65, dam 107," for instance, tells the story. If anybody wants to know more, he turns to No. 76 and No. 107 in the record and thus traces back to the beginning. Pedigree-keeping of late years has grown into cumbersome proportions in the live stock business. By a combination of pedigree and brand, Mr. Sanborn has got rid of about nine-tenths of the labor. He has developed a system which meets all of the practical purposes of pedigrees. For accuracy the small brand beats the description by natural marks all to pieces.

"We have about everything in our favor in North Texas for horse breeding," Mr. Sanborn said in the course of a conversation on the business. "Our climate, water and grass are all right. Our chief concern in breeding

RANCH PETS—THE CHINA GEESE.

here is in regard to temper. We study that with a good deal of care. Much in the way of results depends upon that. By having regard to temper in breeding we find we can greatly reduce the work of breeding and training. We can add to the value of a horse by increasing his amiability. On this place we have been making a study of this feature of breeding, and in our crossing keep it in view as one of the most important conditions. We find that by this study and practice we can obtain control of the question of temper and make a horse of just about the temper we want. I regard this as one of the chief considerations in horse breeding. Yet it is often overlooked. The horsemen will often have in view various other points and combinations in dam and sire, but he will ignore the question of temper. Here we have enough sires to choose from, and can pick to produce good temper."

There are two curiosities on the Sanborn ranch, one living, the other inanimate. In his rambles the superintendent, Mr. Shero, once discovered a pair of China geese. He brought them to Sanborn, and they have the

WAITING TO BE LAUGHED AT.

run of the barn yards, beating watch dogs out of sight, the superintendent says. The China gander, unlike his American cousin, doesn't eat. He has an enormous nose, a double beak as it were, and a great head. He carries that head as high as a very long and a very straight neck will let him. Whenever he sees anybody who is strange or anything which is unusual, he sounds a screeching note of alarm. Geese saved Rome, or some other ancient city, according to history. The Sanborn geese look to be capable of betraying horse-thieves, if they ever have the opportunity.

John Howard, speaking of and for Texas, once proclaimed that there wasn't a cyclone cellar in the State. John Howard isn't often inaccurate, but in this instance he had overlooked the wonderful piece of architecture at Sanborn.

The United States weather service has recently determined, by an elaborate calculation, that Texas, of all of the Western States, has the smallest percentage of cyclones. In fact the percentage is so small that Gen. Greeley recently stated in an address to a scientific society in Washington that Texas might almost be said to be free from these terrible visitations. Notwithstanding this scientific fact, Texas people at one time had something of a scare about cyclones. Looking out upon the limitless prairies, people said to themselves, after reading of disasters outside of their borders: "Well, we'll catch it next. If Kansas and Missouri and Iowa and Nebraska have cyclones, we may as well expect them." Coming from the East, Mr. Sanborn had the Eastern idea of the universality of cyclone dangers in the West. When he laid out the ranch, he didn't stop until he had built a cyclone cellar that is a corker. The cellar is about half above and half under ground. It has an arched roof, and the material is of masonry braced with iron rods an inch and more in thickness. The walls and arch are of 18 inches of solid masonry. The outer surface is plastered with cement. After waiting for a reasonable time to see a cyclone wear itself out on the massive, tomb-like structure, Mr. Sanborn turned the cellar into a dairy house, and it makes a very good one.

The China geese and the cyclone cellar are curiosities. But they are not the most humorous things on the ranch. That distinction belongs to the jackasses. Texas is a wide state and she has room for many things that are comical. But there is nothing funnier than a big group of jacks or jennets and their offspring. Two or three of the big pastures of the Sanborn ranch are given up to these useful but not beautiful animals. Long ears are not an indication of stupidity. They are the badge of patience. They go with a deep and all-pervading spirit of investigation. To stop in the vicinity of these animals is to offer an opportunity for better acquaintance. They cease grazing, big and little come forward to within easy speaking distance, assume a stare of patient interrogation, and wait to be laughed at loud and long. The offspring of jack and jennet seems to come into the world full-grown as to ears, half-grown as to legs and about one-eighth grown as to body. The result is an exaggeration of the grown up oddity. The expression on the countenance is a combination of intelligence, innocence and inquiry, with a suggestion of a considerable capacity for devilment.

W. B. S.

THROUGH TEXAS.

Two Pioneering Phases of the Great Cotton Problem.

The Sherman Experiment—Ups and Downs of Oil Making - The Largest Cotton-Seed Mill in the World—Southern Bags for Northern Grain.

Special Correspondence of the Globe-Democrat.

SHERMAN, TEX., July 21.—There was a time when Texas did not encourage manufacturing. Two Ohio men who came down to furnish the skill for a new enterprise were hung for their hardihood. That was the Tellico incident. Some of the leading citizens of Central Texas got together and agreed that Texas should make her own lumber, grind her own flour and spin her own cotton. They selected Tellico for the location of lumber, flour and cotton manufacturing. They deputized the Hon. Thomas W. McRae to go North and buy the equipment. They contracted with the Ohio men to come down and set the mills going. Mr. McRae started North with the money to buy saws, stones and spindles. On the way he met the eminent statesman of that day, Robert Tombs. Mr. Tombs persuaded McRae that wild land in North Texas was a better thing than cotton manufacturing. Mr. McRae invested in 200,000 acres of land instead of in looms. The Ohio men came down according to contract and went to Tellico to set up the mills. There were no mills to set up. Without waiting to investigate the stories these men told, a mass meeting of Texans decided that the strangers must be abolitionists and hung them. After life was extinct papers arrived from the capitalists who had planned the mills showing the arrangement under which the men had come. Only one of the promoters of the Tellico manufacturing scheme, Judge A. B. Norton, of Dallas, is still living. There are many Texans, not old men, either, who remember very well the unfortunate mistake that was made in the reception of the skilled labor from Ohio.

Things have changed since then. The man who will come to Texas now and start a new industry will get backing and a banquet instead of a rope with a slip-knot. At Sherman the people are a little prouder to-day of a six months' manufacturing experiment than of any other one thing within their community. The experiment is in the manufacture of seamless bags. Raw cotton at the rate of five bales a day is taken from the farmers' wagons at one end of the factory. Finished bags at the rate of 3000 a day are shipped out at the other end. Sherman put $150,000 into this experiment. Supt. Jaques is an Englishman. Asst. Supt. Fairbanks is a Northern man. A fine brick building, with room for double the present capacity of looms, was erected in the outskirts of the city. It is one-story, with great windows letting in all the light and air there is. It stands in the midst of an orchard. Provision is made for pumping in cold air in summer and warm air in winter. The very latest machinery and contrivances, such as automatic feeders for the furnaces and a superb electric light plant, are included in the equipment. Labor is saved at every turn. In the cotton room, where the raw material is received, a picking and breaking machine reduces the staple to sheets. Then comes the carding engine, with its myriads of little teeth, straightening out the fiber. Six rolls pass into one, and are mixed and long drawn out. Next comes a twisting together of strands and more drawing out to get the fiber so distributed that its greatest strength may be obtained. Again and again the strands are mingled and twisted and drawn out until the string which comes from the last mixing represents a portion of each of seventy-two rolls. The next step is the spinning. Three rolls of the string are strung into warp yarn at the rate of $7\frac{1}{4}$ inches of yarn for each inch of the rolls. And now come the looms. By a peculiar double up-and-down movement of the loom, the long seamless bag gradually evolves from the mingling of the countless threads and the flying shuttle when the desired length is reached the shuttle is stopped for a few movements of the loom and then another bag with seamless bottom and seamless sides is begun. The bag comes from the loom completed, with the exception of the turning down of the top edge and a seam by machine to prevent raveling.

space and power to the manufacture of coarse cotton cloth. Only 10, 11 and 12 per cent of the weight of the raw cotton is lost in the process of manufacture, even counting the bale bagging and ties. Cotton costs at the factory 5c and 5½c in these ruinous days. At present prices the thirty bales of bags a day pay a fair return on the investment. But the Sherman people have discovered that the addition of 100 wage-earners to their population of consumers is a good thing all around. They are very well satisfied with their experiment.

The man who shipped the first cotton-seed oil cake to Great Britain lives in Sherman. His name is Capt. Thomas Forbes. He was in the cotton business in New Orleans many years ago. At that time the use of the cotton seed for oil and cake was scarcely known. Somewhere up the country a big planter oc-

THE NEW COTTON BAG FACTORY.

The superintendent of the Sherman factory, after only six months running, lays down the bags of Manchester, N. H., beside those from his own looms, and invites comparison by microscope.

"I will leave it to any unprejudiced person to say if our bags do not show better cotton and better workmanship," he said. Drawing through his fingers a fragment from a roll until the fiber slowly parted, he added: "There; you can't beat that staple anywhere. It is over an inch long. The finest cotton in the United States grows along Red River from Sherman to Paris."

The Sherman bag factory has been running six months. Its product has gone as far East as Cincinnati, as far North as St. Paul. The officers of the company are satisfied. The orders ahead call for steady running until October. The company will either double the machinery for bag making or apply the surplus

casionally ground a few hundred bushels of seed in a rude way, and sent it in the form of oil cake down to New Orleans. "I had seen some of these small lots of cake," said Capt. Forbes, "and it struck me the cake might be used to fatten cattle in Great Britain. An English gentleman was visiting in New Orleans about that time. I told him of the cake and what I thought could be done with it. He said he had never seen anything of the kind, and was quite curious about it. I told him I'd send over some, but when I came to get the cake I discovered that it was harder to do than I had thought. By picking up a small lot here and a small lot there, I collected forty or fifty tons and sent it over. The business proved to be very profitable. Some of the scientific men on the other side took hold of the cake and analyzed it. They said, ' Here we can get more oil out of it than the Yankees do.' So they got up machinery, subjected the oil cake to another process and then fed the cake to their cattle. It was in 1846 I made this first shipment of oil cake to Great Britain. The business was even at that time profitable. But it is only in the last fifteen years or so that the oil and cake from the cotton seed has come into such general use. When I first came to Texas to live there wasn't a bale of cotton shipped out of the State. Now Texas sells 2,000,000 bales."

"And the great addition Texas has made to the cotton supply is the cause of the low prices, isn't it, Captain?"

"Partly that is the cause. But people don't use as much cotton as they did. The cotton goods made now lasts longer than that manufactured formerly. That is one of the principal reasons why there is overproduction of cotton now."

Mr. Tassey started in a very modest way. The first thing we knew about him he was making oil out there. He kept on independently increasing his plant and business. After he had made an eminent success of it we formed a stock company and backed him with all the money he wanted. But J. C. Tassey is entitled to the credit of giving Sherman the largest oil mill in the South and the largest cotton gin in the world. And now we are building an entirely new mill, which will have a front of 300 feet and will contain the finest machinery that can be devised. We are building with brick and stone and in the most substantial manner. But brick and stone and machinery

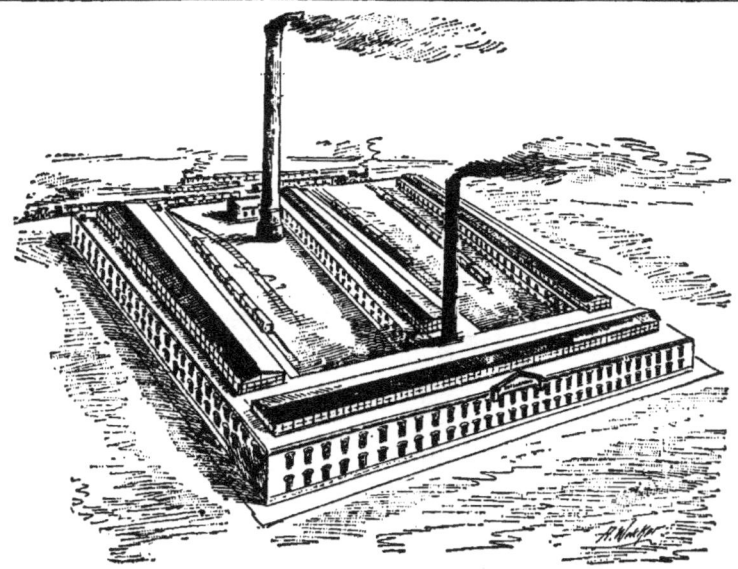

THE LARGEST COTTON-SEED OIL MILL IN THE WORLD.

The largest cotton-seed mill in the world is rising from its foundations on the prairie east of Sherman. It will eat up 432 tons of cotton-seed in twenty-four hours. That means the seed which grows with over 800 bales of cotton. A half ton of seed to a bale of cotton is the average. Something more than a dozen years ago a young Pittsburger, who had had a good schooling in machinery and its uses, came to Sherman and started a little seed mill in the outskirts of the city.

"That," said banker Randolph, one of the solid capitalists of Sherman, "was almost before we, who had been here a lifetime, knew there was such a thing as oil in cotton seed.

do not make a successful cotton-seed mill. That takes brains. We rely on Mr. Tassey to furnish them."

The banker's reference to brains is full of meaning. There has been a great deal of money made in the cotton-seed oil manufacture in Texas. There has been a great deal lost. A few years ago, after a very good season for the business, there was an epidemic of oil mill investment in the State. Every large town in the cotton producing parts of Texas had its mill. There were no fewer than thirty of these enterprises. A bad year sent two-thirds of them to the wall. Last season was a good one for those mills which survived in Texas. And now there is another epidemic of oil mill building likely to be followed by another assortment of wrecks. In the manufacture of cotton-seed oil men play for big stakes. Few products are so fluctuating in price as those which come out of a cotton-seed oil mill. The Sherman mill has sold oil at 55c and oil at 20c. It has sold oil cake at $20 a ton and oil cake at $10 a ton.

"The size of the cotton crop," Mr. Tassey explained, in the course of an interesting conversation about this peculiar industry, "has nothing to do with it. The market is speculative. In 1882 we had a good year, one of the best. In 1887 we had a fairly prosperous season. Last year was good. The elements of uncertainty in the business are men. Last year, for example, we had good crops in this country. In Europe the crops failed. There was a great demand for our oil cake for feeding, and we sold at profitable prices. Practically all of the oil cake goes abroad. This year Europe has good cereal crops and a good root crop. She will not need so much oil cake as she did last year, and she will not pay so much for what she does take. There are other conditions which enter into this business. A big corn crop in this country means a big hog crop. That means lots of grease and less demand for cotton-seed oil. The most of our oil product goes into the manufacture of compound lard. When the hog crop is large the oil man has to scratch his head to think how he will pull through. We have to commence buying and working up cotton-seed before we know what the hog crop is going to be and what the demand for oil will be. Thus, before we know what our margin will be we are in the midst of our season. Then there are years when the seed rots on our hands. For some climatic reason the seed will not keep some seasons as it does others. I have seen $150,000 worth of seed lost by Texas mills in a single year, just because it would not keep until it could be worked up."

"Does cotton seed grade like cotton?"

"The staple has little to do with the seed. The seed on the Texas uplands is not as good as that raised in the Mississippi bottoms. It is not as rich in oil. But beyond these differences there is not much relationship between the staple and the seed."

"How much of the cotton seed raised in Texas goes to the oil mills, Mr. Tassey?"

"Not to exceed 20 per cent. But all goes that can be handled profitably. At least one-third of the seed must be saved over for the next year's crop. You know the planter is obliged to save not only enough for seeding once, but also enough for a second seeding. Cotton must be replanted occasionally. Then there is a good deal of seed at such a distance from mills that it will not pay to haul and ship. About 20 per cent I think is all there is of the cotton seed raised in Texas which can be handled with profit to the raiser to the mills. Last year, with some of the Texas mills closed by the trust, there were still enough running in Texas to take all of the seed that could be handled profitably in this State."

"What will these twelve or fifteen new mills do?"

Mr. Tassey shook his head.

"If the mills don't make money, their competition will make better prices for the planter, won't it?"

"That is a mistake. It isn't for the interest of the farmer to have too many seedmen handling his crop. Taxes, interest and other expenses increase with the number of mills. That means an increased burden for the industry to carry. There is only about so much seed to be ground up. The more mills and the more investment the less there is left for the farmer. If you argue, as the men with machinery to sell are telling, that more mills will increase the amount of seed bought and manufactured into oil, you reach the same result. There is a market for about so much oil and cake, and when there is increased production the prices go down and there is less to be paid to the farmer for his seed. There are mills enough now to do the business. The increase of mills will, it seems to me, mean a decrease in the prices paid for seed. The machinery men figure out a different showing, but they are interested in equipping as many mills as they can."

"But you are building a large mill, Mr. Tassey?"

"We are not building to increase our capacity, but to increase our facilities for handling and to reduce cost. We expect to manufacture what we do now, but we expect to do it in much less time. Quick handling of the seed is necessary to success with it. We shall cut down the chances of loss from seed spoiling on our hands, and we shall get our product into market quicker. That is the idea on which we are constructing our new mill."

All is not gold that glitters in the cotton-seed oil business. For instance, there is the oil-cake feeding in this country. Some Texas cattlemen builded great expectations on the results of the early experiments.

"Under present conditions there is no money either to the mill or to the cattlemen in feeding cake here," Mr. Tassey said. "I believe that every cattleman who has taken it up and followed it has lost. Two years ago cattle which were fattened on oil cake yielded a profit. That was on account of the high price of beef cattle. Last year the balance was the other way. There were men who fed 3,000 head of cattle here, but they made nothing."

"How was that, Mr. Tassey?"

"The range men got it all. The men who fed $16 a ton for their meal. They sold their cattle at 2¾c and 3c fattened. The trouble was they put the cattle in at $20 a head from the range. That was too high to leave a margin of profit at the low price for beef cattle. The year before that the feeders put in their cattle at $20 or $25 from the range, paid about the same price for meal as last year, but sold for 4½c. That gave a margin of profit."

"So far as the fattening goes, oil cake is all right?"

"Cotton-seed meal and bulls make the finest fattening food that can be given cattle. At the average prices they will fatten cattle cheaper than corn at 20c a bushel. But there must be a better balance between range and fed cattle than there has been to make this kind of feeding profitable."

Returns from the cotton acreage of North Texas show a decrease of 25 per cent as compared with last year. For the rest of the State the decrease is not quite so much. The average for the whole State is about 20 per cent. This reduction of acreage is in a degree more apparent than real. Last year's cotton crop in Texas was extraordinary in acreage and yield. The reduction of 25 per cent this year is in reality only about 10 per cent under two years ago. Low prices and the agitation over the cotton grower's condition prompted the North Texans to cut off one-fourth of their cotton ground and put it into corn and other grain.

But Mr. Tassey doesn't believe the Texas cotton-grower's condition is as bad as it has been pictured. "Last year's cotton crop," he said, "was marketed at only about 8 per cent below the average price for ten years. I mean that in North Texas the man who picked and sold his cotton immediately came within 8 per cent of the average price for the whole ten years preceding."

Some surprise was expressed at this as being rather inconsistent with the popular impression about the hard lot of the cotton farmer.

"I am not talking about the man who held on to his cotton until it went down to 6½c and 6c," Mr. Tassey continued. And then he made another point even more surprising. He said: "We figured this out, taking all of the recent twenty years except 1881, which we left out because it was exceptional on account of a very small crop and very high prices. But our cotton raisers more than made up for the 8 per cent loss in average price by the increased yield per acre. Cotton in North Texas when sold right after picking paid more per acre the past season than the average cotton crop for ten years. The average yield was from 15 to 20 per cent better than the average for nine or ten years. Most of those who sold promptly got 8c. We bought cotton here right along up to the time our gin burned in October and we did not pay under 8c. Of course, those who held cotton and saw it go down to 6½c and 8c were badly hurt. Some farmers held on, hoping for better prices, and got pinched. The merchants were hurt worse than the farmers. They were left with the declining cotton on their hands. They were forced to ask extensions from those with whom they dealt North. They pleaded the low price of cotton and said the farmers could not pay up, and out of all this talk grew the impression that the actual cotton grower was a great deal worse off than he really was. You can easily figure how much the grower can afford to stand in decrease of price if he gets 15 to 20 per cent increase of yield per acre. Then there is the matter of supply. The decline in what the farmer buys has been much more than in the cotton he sells. Clothing, sugar, coffee, machinery, all have decreased in price in greater percentage than cotton has. The fact is the cotton-grower's condition in Texas is better than is generally supposed. The bad impression is largely due to the merchants who got caught by the decline of cotton, and who, in asking extension from Northern creditors, made it appear that the farmer had lost money on his crop and couldn't pay. I didn't say there is money in cotton at present prices, but the Texas farmer who sold promptly did not lose money last season."

"Don't you think the Texas farmer will be better off with less cotton and more corn?"

"Cotton is the selling crop for Texas farmers for this reason. A large corn crop down here makes a cheap corn crop. An increase of 100 per cent in the Texas corn crop will depreciate the price 50 per cent. Cotton, in 1883, the year of a great crop, sold for 8½c. It has depreciated but 25 per cent since, taking the lowest price. As I said before, the Texas farmer made more money last year per acre on cotton than he has made in the average of the ten previous years. When we raise a large corn crop we can't feed it all. Corn, oats and hay have only a local market. The cotton crop has the world for a market. It will hold its price better than any of these other products."

"What the South mostly needs," said Mr. Tassey, "is manufactures of cotton. I could talk to you all night about that, or I could tell you my opinion in a sentence. To put it the shortest way I would say, 'For a man of enterprise with sufficient experience and capital, who wants a stable, legitimate business, the manufacture of cotton goods in the South presents to-day the finest opportunity in the United States.' I don't say it is a field for an old fogy with set notions, but for a man with good business ideas and energy. Cotton manufacturing is a business that is bound to come South. We shall have to begin with coarse goods. That was what New England did. Great Britain thought years ago that coarse cotton goods couldn't be made in New England, but American mills succeeded. Now they are making the finer goods, not the finest, but finer grades. The history of cotton manufacture in New England will repeat itself in the South. New England manufacturers think we haven't the labor. We shall have it. We shall educate labor to the work, just as was done in New England. We have got to start in with the coarser goods. We shall manufacture just as cheaply from the labor standpoint. We shall have the advantage of saving the cost of transportation on the raw material all the way to New England, and for our local market we shall save the cost of the transportation of the manufactured goods from New England to Texas. The manufacture of cotton goods is certain to come to the South." W. B. S.

THROUGH TEXAS.

The Progress of the "Nester" Across the Panhandle Pastures.

Symptoms of a Healthy Reaction—The Story of the Cowman's Bluff— A Prairie-Dog Problem.

Special correspondence of the Globe-Democrat.

IN THE PANHANDLE, TEXAS, August 2.— The Panhandle has raised another grain crop. The figures are not all in. But the estimate at the Fort Worth Board of Trade is a crop of 6,500,000 bushels of wheat. Oats and barley will go 3,000,000 more. As for the corn, that is beyond guessing. Gen. Clark, of the Fort Worth Board of Trade, said: "The corn crop of Texas this year will be phenomenal. We have thousands of acres that will give seventy-five bushels to the acre."

On the Hoxie farm, near Taylor, in Williamson County, Central Texas, there have just been threshed out 30,000 bushels of oats, and there will be 70,000 bushels of corn. The rest of the country does not know how rapidly Texas is forging ahead as a grain State. Not one out of a hundred Texans appreciate what is going on in this direction. Who ever heard of Texas barley? Last winter a Fort Worth man went around and induced some of the farmers to try barley. One of them, a Mr.

GATEWAY TO THE PANHANDLE—THE FORT WORTH BOARD OF TRADE.

Clanahan, put in 500 acres. He has harvested his crop, and it yields him $24 per acre, or $12,000 on his experiment. A malthouse is being built at Fort Worth, and 500,000 bushels of barley are wanted for the first year. The Hoxie farm will put in 500 acres of this new grain for Texas next season. The average yield of barley in the experimental fields this year has been fifty bushels, and the St. Louis price is being paid in Fort Worth; where the grain is wanted for home consumption.

THE PANHANDLE "NESTER."

This is not a good grain year for Texas. It is the poorest in five years. In the Panhandle the wheat crop is spoken of as a failure. That is because the Panhandle farmer considers anything less than twelve bushels a failure. The season has been erratic in Texas as it has been in other parts of the country. Some farmers have got eight bushels; some have got fifteen bushels. Here and there a report of the threshing shows twenty and twenty-five bushels. But the average is lower than it has been for the five years which have elapsed since the discovery of the grain-growing capacity of the Panhandle. And so these farmers call it a failure.

That jog of Texas which runs up north between Indian Territory on the east and New Mexico on the west is the Panhandle proper. It is larger than most States. By common consent the name has been extended to the great body of chocolate-colored loam which constitutes the red lands. The Panhandle, as originally applied, was a day's ride from Fort Worth. The Panhandle as comprehended to-day is reached a couple of hours after leaving "The Fort." And then the traveler is in it for the rest of the day and most of the night.

The revolution in the Panhandle has been a quick one. The first thresher brought into the new wheat country was an old ten horse-power from Illinois. It is still running near Wichita Falls. The man who came on with this thresher says that the first year after his arrival he didn't find a field which yielded less than seventeen bushels an acre. He did the threshing for a whole county. That was six years ago. This season it was possible to see eight reapers marching en echelon across one wheat field in the same county. The farmer who furnished such a pageant had 1,500 acres in wheat out of 4,000 acres for which he paid $10 an acre. Up and down the Wichita Valley, which is part of this new wheat country, can be seen ascending the smoke of a score of steam threshers, although this is a failure season. At Wichita Falls there are three flouring mills and three elevators. One of these mills turns out 500 barrels of flour a day. A new mill of 200 barrels capacity and a new elevator of 100,000 bushels room are nearing completion to help take care of a crop which is a failure. Last year these mills at Wichita Falls ran night and day from harvest to harvest. And then enough wheat to have kept three such mills running was shipped away. In two months last year the farmers of adjoining counties received $750,000 at Vernon for the wheat they hauled in.

"In 1867," said Mr. L. P. Goodell, a Fort Worth business man, "I went into Minnesota. When I came to Texas I thought I had never seen two countries look so much alike as Minnesota and the Panhandle, before either had been developed. You know they used to say in those days we couldn't raise anything in Minnesota, just as they said only five years ago no crops would grow in the Panhandle."

Here was a strong motive for the assertion that the Panhandle would not grow crops.

HARVESTING ON THE KNOTT FARM IN THE PANHANDLE.

When the Comanche moved out of this region the cowman moved in. He had great influence in Texas at that time. He could go to Austin and convince the State government that whole counties in the Panhandle should be classified as grazing land. The law of the State limits the buyer of agricultural land to a section, a mile square. But it allows the buyer of grazing land to buy in his own name seven sections upon extremely favorable terms, and it doesn't raise any technicality if every member of the family also takes seven sections. The cowmen took possession of the Panhandle. They bought in blocks of seven, at 50c and $1 an acre. The school lands which they couldn't buy they leased from the State and fenced in with their great pastures. Then came along the man with a hoe. He looked at the red lands, chocolate-colored when moist and like brick dust when dry. He manifested an inclination to stir up the soil and see what it would do. The cowmen resented this as an intrusion. They called the man with the hoe "a nester." That was because he would buy a piece of the school land and settle right down in the middle of a big pasture, making it necessary to allow roadways and to build gates for him. As the Comanche felt toward the cowman, so the cowman felt toward the nester. But it was evolution. The cowman might frighten the nester away to-day. The next day there were two men with hoes looking over the same wire fence. The two men might be induced by argument to believe that there was nothing in it for them. On the third day four men with hoes were at the barbed-wire fence. The cowboys whooped it up pretty lively for the original nester. The cowman argued and made discouraging laws for the two nesters. When the four men with hoes arrived, the cowman hired smooth talkers to help convince them that agriculture was impossible in the Panhandle. Perhaps this is the only

THE 500-BARREL MILL AT WICHITA FALLS.

new country where such efforts were made to keep people out. Men received salaries to tell newcomers that farming was impossible. They made it their business for pay to discourage immigration. Strangers on the trains and in the new towns were sought out. They were told that nothing would grow, and if anything did grow the prairie dogs would eat it up. This wasn't a very good article of logic. Perhaps the man with the hoe thought so. At any rate, he wasn't altogether convinced. He hung around. He said he'd give the red land a whirl. As for the prairie dog, the man with the hoe said that while waiting for his first crop he would make war on that festive little animal which sat upon its hind legs and laughed a file-scraping "he-he-he" at him as he went by. If the tickling of the soil hadn't turned out better than the war on the prairie dog, the Panhandle wouldn't be crossed and cris-crossed by wheat fields to-day. The idea of the man with the hoe was to sell the skins of the prairie dogs to the glove manufacturer and the canned meat to Chinamen. The New York glove manufacturer accepted one consignment of skins and quit. The Chinaman declined the meat with a "no moochee." The prairie dog industry suddenly and severely languished.

But the experiment with the soil—that was altogether different. The Wichita Valley is a part of the Panhandle. From the Wichita River stretches a bottom several miles wide and as level as the famous Red River Valley of the North. In this valley was made the notable experiment which knocked out the cowmen's double-barreled argument. John Howard put in 400 acres of oats, corn and millet. The result was a crop which startled the whole Panhandle. The prairie dogs didn't eat half an acre of the 400. In fact they showed their disgust at the turned-over sod and moved on, thereby setting the cowmen

THE MAN WITH A HOE.

a lesson. Not one prairie dog is seen now where there were a thousand before. The season following the object lesson everybody went to planting. The 400 acres bought for $5 an acre was sold for $13. It was divided into smaller farms and sold again for $20. A couple of years after the experimental crop came the discovery that the red lands with a world of gypsum underneath was a natural wheat country. That settled the issue between the cowman and the man with a hoe. In the picturesque language of a pioneer, "it decided that the Panhandle was to be no longer the land of the longhorns and h—ll."
W. B. S

THROUGH TEXAS.

Twenty-Bushel Wheat in Place of Twenty-Acre Cow Brute.

A Cattle King's Testimony—Panhandle Surprises—The Romance of Grain Farming.

Special Correspondence of the Globe-Democrat.

IN THE PANHANDLE OF TEXAS, August 3.— Charles Goodnight is the greatest of the Panhandle cattle kings. His ranch is far beyond the red lands where wheat grows. It is up in the Panhandle proper, upon the Staked Plains. But the tide of farming immigration has flowed almost to the Goodnight pastures.

"Can a farmer make a living as far West as this?" Mr. Goodnight was asked.

The cattle king was here even before the Comanches went out. He has seen some thirty summers come and go in the Panhandle. He deliberated a little before answering the question, and then he said:

acre. He has seen the free grass disappear and the wire fences extend like a great web all over the plains. He has had to drive his herds hundreds of miles to the nearest shipping point. He now has a railroad station in his front door yard. When he gets on the cars at Fort Worth he rides through a succession of towns and cities which five years ago had no existence, or at best were only trading posts.

Twenty bushels of wheat to the acre is what the Panhandle farmers claim this land will produce in good seasons. John W. Carhart, one of the leading men of Clarendon, sat upon the vine-covered porch of the Goodnight place and said: "The poorest yield of wheat around Clarendon last year was 12 bushels to the acre. I remember one field of 160 acres which gave 3000 bushels. The average crop is about 20 bushels. But I think the best results will be obtained out here on the edge of the Staked Plains by combining some stock-raising with farming. There is a belt of country extending fifty miles east from the eastern verge of the plains. It has a southeastern exposure. There are vast numbers of springs. One county, Donley, has at least 1000 of them. This belt presents the finest conditions for doing farming that I know of anywhere. I am from the dairy region of Wisconsin, and I know just what that development has been. I can say that I believe in this spring belt along

"CHUCK IN"

"Yes, a farmer can make a living out here. But he can't make money. He may, by hard work, do a little better some seasons than a living, but he can't get rich. The only way a farmer can do well here is to combine stock-raising with his farming."

"Mr. Goodnight, how much pasture land do you allow for each animal?"

"Twenty acres."

Mr. Goodnight has seen land in the Panhandle go from nothing to 50c an acre. He has seen the 50c land advance to $3 and $5 an

the Staked Plains, which, ten years ago, we were taught to believe was a desert. There are finer conditions for dairying than Wisconsin possesses. This short dry grass gives a butter that is better flavored than any you ever tasted. People from the blue grass and clover dairying country say so. And the conditions are such that butter can be made easier here in this clear dry atmosphere. The creeks of the springs region are set with grapes and plums. Ten thousand gallons of wine goes to waste. In the season when grapes are ripe the ground along the creeks is blue. Plums are hauled into Clarendon by the wagon load. I don't know of a season since I have been here that this natural fruit has failed.''

The Panhandle is full of surprises, and Mr. Carhart's testimony to the existence of this natural dairy country on the edge of the Staked Plains is one of them.

This transformation of the Panhandle is an agricultural revolution. The wonder is that so little has been said about it. When the wheat producing quality of North Dakota lands was discovered the whole world was told. Dalrymple's farm was talked about, described in print and painted on canvas. The Red River Valley of the North became a place for pilgrimages. Well, there is a Red River Valley of the South, and how many people know of it, except as a region where the slaves of King Cotton toil sixteen hours a day with the hoe, the cultivator and the patient mule? But that is not the Red River Valley of the South, of which the Panhandle supply. So it appears that the four successive good crops of wheat in the Panhandle were not accidents.

Wheat-raising is as easy as improved methods can make it in the Panhandle. At Vernon, one of the smartest of these brand new cities, there were sold last season 547 self-binders. The steam threshing outfits are now sweeping through the fields. It takes a force of twenty-five men and ten teams to run one of these outfits, while steam-power does the actual threshing. The wheat-raiser has nothing to do but to open the gate when the outfit arrives and to take care of the grain as it comes from the spout in a golden stream. It matters not to the threshing boss whether the grain is in shock or in stack. Not one in twenty of the Panhandle grain-growers puts the sheaves in stack. Perhaps it would be better for the grain if it was done. But the threshing outfit includes the men and teams to gather in the grain from the shock. The extra charge for threshing in that way is only 2c a bushel on wheat and 1c on oats. So the Panhandle farmer relieves

THE ROMANCE OF GRAIN-GROWING.

is part. A geological map of Texas has as many colors as Joseph's coat. Just below the western half of the Indian Territory this map shows a great patch of the color of brick dust. It is "the red lands" in scientific lingo. The red lands is a natural wheat country, as much so as the Red River Valley of the North, and the dead levels of the eastern half of North Dakota. There is more of the red lands in square miles than there is of the North Dakota wheat region. Chemistry explains the practical results of wheat-growing in the red lands. The gypsum and the other properties which wheat wants are here in extraordinary himself of one of the most tedious features of grain raising. The threshing boss, like Miles Standish, knows every man in his army and divides up the work with system. Eight of the ten teams haul the sheaves from the field to thresher. To one team is assigned the duty of keeping water in the boiler, and to another is given the work of hauling fuel. A most important part of the outfit is the boarding house on wheels. It is an airy-looking structure. The sides are open and the roof is of canvas. A cook stove occupies a corner, and the table accommodations seat the whole party. Most of the threshers are farmers' lads from the surrounding country. They make quick and merry work of what used to be the most anxious event of the year on the grain farm. The new way is a great change from the old. There is no more rallying of neighbors to exchange threshing work. Housewives do not work a week preparing for the threshers and another week clearing up after them. The farmer counts his bushels and pays at the rate of 8c for wheat and 4c for oats. The threshing outfit does the rest.

such manifestations of popular sentiment. A faint echo of the whoop reaches "the chuck wagon" on the other side of the field handy to the water. The cook and his assistants quicken their movements between the stove and the table. The boss looks at his watch and at the sun. He takes a hasty survey of the field. He gives no signal. Every man sticks to his post and the work goes on. A quarter of an hour passes. The warning whoop is heard again. Once more the boss

PANHANDLE PRODUCTS AND THE MEN WHO GROW THEM.

When the sun is nearly overhead a shout goes up from some part of the busy scene. It is a genuine Texas whoop, high-keyed and piercing. Then another answers. From away down in the field where a wagon is loading comes a third yell. And after a few moments a whole chorus arises. All of this is by way of intimation to the boss that noontime approaches. He is a wise boss who heeds

looks at his watch. Then he walks over to the engine and the whistle answers the whoop with a toot. Work stops instanter. Steam is turned off. The belt is dropped. Teams are unhitched. There is a race across the field for the chuck wagon. Some men are at the table as soon as they can climb into the wagon. Others move with more deliberation, stopping to feed a team or to wash themselves.

There is a good deal of human nature in a threshing outfit. Meantime the first comers sit about the loaded, smoking table, but not so much as a crust of bread is broken. The lines along the board fill in. Still nobody starts. Now and then a warning cry of "Chuck in" is heard, but nobody "chucks in." All are seated but one man engaged on a more elaborate toilet than the others have made. "Chuck in!" "Chuck in!" comes the warning again. "Go ahead!" responds the dude as he raises a piece of looking glass and moves his head to one side and then the other. The threshers take him at his word and bread is broken all along the table. A good commissary is as important as the water in the boiler for a threshing outfit. When darkness comes the threshers lie down upon little heaps of straw in the stubble, with the Milky Way for a coverlet. Out-of-door sleeping is no hardship in the Panhandle country. Thousands do it as a matter of comfort and preference. No dew worth mentioning falls. A steady dry breeze blows from the South. Such a thing as a cold caught in this way is almost unknown. The largest cattle king in the Panhandle has an upper room in his house with three sides left open, and there he spends the most of his summer nights. All through the Panhandle cots and shake-downs may be seen outside of the houses. Camping is a luxury in this climate.

While his men ate a threshing boss told his story. "My name is Heagle," he said, "and I am from Algiers. One day ten of us came to Wichita Falls. We couldn't speak a word of English. We had just $9 among us. Our intention was to go to Wilbarger County, but the Wichita River was up, and while we waited for it to go down we arranged to take some land on shares. From that we made enough to buy two sections of land at $5 an acre. On that land we made $6,000 worth of crops. We have sold our land for $20 an acre and are going into the next county to get cheaper land and start again. We are worth $15,000 apiece, and every dollar of it except the $9 that was in the party when we came here has been made in the Panhandle. Noboby could get me to leave the Panhandle."

It is four parts romance and luck with one part work, this grain growing in the Panhandle. With six mules and a gang plow the farmer turns a wide strip of the red lands every trip across the field. There were sold 108 of these big gang plows in a single Panhandle town this season. And with these went 260 drills. The Panhandle farmer quadruples the work of the old single furrow; he rides his drill and his work is done until the ripening grain calls for the binder, which

A PANHANDLE CIVILIZER.

drops the sheaves by half dozens. Shocking is the only hand work. Then comes the threshing outfit, leaving to the farmer nothing more to do but to haul his product to the nearest town. With such methods explained the stories told on the Panhandle are not so incredible. For instance, it is related that one man and a boy 16 years old produced 10,000 bushels of grain in a single season. Such methods and such a country where the gang plow can run every month in the year, tell the reason why there is no more "dollar wheat." It isn't option trading that is knocking the bottom out of prices. The Panhandle has only just begun. It hasn't struck its gait as a grain-producing region. Five years hence, look out for the Panhandle.

The people of Wichita Falls preserve three pictures illustrating their three eras. In the first picture there are two log houses on a prairie. That was the first era. On the second picture is a single street, a row of saloons and a group of cowboys. That is the second era. The third picture is a bird's-eye view of a well-built city of 4,000 people, with a big court house and a bigger school house, church spires, mills and elevators, $7,000 residences, a wholesale grocery doing a business of $50,000 a month, and other things to match. The three eras are embraced in a decade. In 1887 Wichita Falls had 400 voters. In 1889 she had 800 voters. In 1892 she has 1,600 voters. Five years ago a good month's business for the railroad station was $5,000. Now it is from $50,000 to $80,000. The idea of making the school house larger than the court house is purely Panhandle. The court house hobby may not be of Texas origin, but it finds strong development here. A Texas county seat which hasn't a big court house isn't satisfied until it gets one. And the more brick and mortar and cupola that can be heaped up the happier is the community. There probably isn't another State in the Union which has so many court houses and so much money invested in court house architecture in proportion to wealth and population. But the Panhandle is New Texas. When Wichita Falls got ready to build something to astonish the natives, she put up a $25,000 school house on a fine square in the very center of the city. She provided for nine months of free school. After that she built a substantial Court House, but it isn't as large as the school house. The Panhandle theory is that if the school house is large the community will not need such a fine court house. There are parts of Texas where not so very long ago it took nerve to advocate free schools for more than three months. It takes nerve now in the Panhandle not to advocate free schools for nine months.

The Panhandle abounds in ambitious towns. Just beyond Wichita Falls is Iowa Park. Less than five years ago two Iowa men came down here prospecting. One of them, Mr. Kolp, had been Speaker of the Iowa House of Representatives. The other, Mr. Kennedy, had been a member of the same body. They found a body of school lands, 17,000 acres, which belonged to Tarrant County. This tract they acquired at from $4 to $6 an acre. In 1888 they laid out a town. Four years ago there wasn't a house on the site, and now there are 1,200 people, with a mill, a couple of elevators and brick business blocks. The grain elevator is as much a feature of the Panhandle towns as it is of the North Dakota community. Vernon, Quanah, Childress, Memphis, Clarendon, Washburn, Amarillo, and even the smaller towns between have prepared to handle grain. Many of these towns are even younger than Iowa Park. Several are healthy infants of two years' and eighteen months' growth. W. B. S.

THROUGH TEXAS.

How the Newest City of the Panhandle Got a Move on Itself.

A Lone Court House—Tarrant County's Campaign of Education—Old Texas —Greer County to the Front.

Special Correspondence of the Globe-Democrat.

IN THE PANHANDLE OF TEXAS, August 5.— Amarillo is the newest of the Panhandle cities. The waiter at the Hotel asks you if you will have your eggs "standing up." You pay the gentlemanly "barkeep" 15c for a glass of pop if the imposing analysis of the water scares you. The water comes from a depth of over 200 feet, and is raised by windmills, which on the plains can be guaranteed to run twenty-three hours out of the twenty-four, and about 364 days in the year. The water looks and tastes all right. Nobody ever experienced any ill results from it. But in an evil hour somebody had it analyzed and paraded the analysis in big type as a thing to be proud of. When the newcomer reads all about the potassium and the sodium and the sulphur he steers forthwith for one of the six saloons in a single block of the main street, and invests 15c in a quarter-of-a-cent's worth of pop. The saloon business is a great industry in Amarillo and will continue to be so long as the saloon trust continues.

Young as she is, Amarillo has had two sites. The original town company located on a slope two miles west of where the town now stands. About 1200 people established themselves there. As is usual in Texas and some other countries, the first thing the new community did when it felt its strength was to vote about $25,000 for a court house. This was expected to anchor the county seat and the town for all time to come. The Court House was built, and a good one it is for the money.

But a man who owns a pasture of 250,000 acres decided that the town had been put in the wrong place. It was in "a draw." The right location was two miles further east on an eligible elevation. To the proposition to move the town said "no." The pasture man went ahead and laid out a new site. He built a hotel that was bigger and cost 50 per cent more than the Court House. For a few weeks there was an interesting game of tug between Court House and hotel two miles apart. According to Texas tradition the Court House should have won. A county seat is located by vote on a specified section of land for five years, and there it must stay till the last day of the fifth year. The pasture man was from the North. He said he was willing to spend

$100,000 to put Amarillo where it belonged, and he did it. After he had built his big hotel —big for this region—he bought the hotel in the original Amarillo, put it on wheels, moved it over to the new site, located it across a little park, and called it the annex. The pasture man's father-in-law is an Illinois barb-wire millionaire. He came down and looked on. He said he didn't know much about town-site wars, but he would back the new location. The pasture man dug wells and built houses. Every week or two he drove over to old Amarillo, bought a store, put it on wheels and hauled it over to new Amarillo. There was no shouting or hurrahing. But month by month the old town melted away and the new town grew. To-day the Court House is all that marks the original site. It stands alone on the prairie. It can't be moved under the law.

eral miles of mains. Amarillo, to begin with, was essentially a stockmen's town, but the inevitable man with the hoe has arrived and is disposed to see what he can do. The Campbellite minister, who moved to the Panhandle from near Sedalia, Mo., a garden spot if there is one on the footstool, came into town one day this week with beards of wheat all over him.

"What have you been doing, brother?" a church member asked.

"Threshing my wheat," replied the minister triumphantly.

"How much did it go?" asked the member.

"Sixty bushels," said the minister.

"Wha-at?" ejaculated the brother.

"I mean sixty bushels on the eight acres," explained the minister, with a laugh. "But I lost at least two bushels an acre by letting it get too ripe. I'm not discouraged. I raised

AMARILLO—SKETCHED FROM DEPOT.

If it could be, the father of the new town would have moved it long ago. The county officers walk two miles to the Court House and back again every day. As they go over in the morning they often see a beautiful mirage—houses, trees, lakes and the shadows of a city. When they get to the Court House the vision fades and there is nothing but bare prairie and the holes where the houses stood.

The end of the fifth year approaches, and the fate of the lone Court House is already determined. A square in the center of new Amarillo has been set apart for a new and larger county seat anchor. The old Court House, brick, mortar and all, will be put on wheels and hauled to the new town. When wings shall have been added it will become a college.

The pasture man is self-willed, but he is something of a philanthropist. He has given the new town a water works system with sev-

this in a bad season on ground which had the sod turned only last year. I'm going to sow again this fall. We'll raise wheat in Potter County yet. I'm told there are 50,000 bushels of wheat that would be marketed right here in Amarillo if we only had a mill."

The Frying Pan ranch comes right up to the edge of Amarillo. In it are 250,000 acres. The owner has recently said to his agent: "I won't stand in the way of settlers. They can have the land if they want it. When Texas land was selling at $2 an acre and money could be borrowed at 6 and 8 per cent, I was a buyer. Now that land is worth $4, I am a seller. I have made more money, perhaps, than I am entitled to." During the summer this man has sold over twenty sections of 640 acres each in various counties of the Panhandle for $4 an acre. There came an order this week from Denver for a section at $2.50 an acre, to be within ten miles of Amarillo. The real estate agents couldn't fill it. Amarillo is Spanish. It should be pronounced Am-a-re-o. The inhabitants are Americans, and they adhere to the American pronunciation.

Up and down the Panhandle the Texans are praying that the title of Greer County may be vested in the United States. This may sound strange to those who know how proud Texans are of their State's bigness. Greer County is either the southwestern corner of Indian Territory, or else it is the elbow of the Panhandle. The United States claims Greer county. So does Texas. She has recognized the county organization which the squatters have set up. In conventions and in other formal ways Greer County is conceded representation. But this is pending a decison as to the ownership. All Texas maps show the State line running around to the north of Greer. All United States maps trace the Texas boundary south of Greer. The sole question is which is Red River? Red River divides Indian Territory from Texas. There is no dispute as to where the river runs until the forks are reached. Texas insists that one fork is the main river. The United States considers the other fork the main river. And it makes just the difference of Greer County which is right. Greer lies between the forks. Forty-six years ago the independent Republic of Texas was annexed to the United States. Nobody at that time had ever heard of Greer County. The issue of the forks of Red River had not been raised. Some time in the remote past a boundary commission went up Red River. The work was done in such an ill-defined way that it left the opportunity for a question about which fork was treated as the main river. So long as nobody wanted Greer County land neither the United States nor Texas manifested much interest in settling the fork problem. But after the Comanches were corraled on a reservation and the cowmen divided up, the Panhandle squatters began to drift in-between the forks of the Red.

The American creates government wherever he goes. No matter how new or isolated the settlement, the next thing after the staking out of the claims is the erection of some form

COWBOYS AT LUNCH.

of organization which will give semblance of stability to title and which will insure law and order. Foreign anarchists and Socialists run up against this strong American trait and surprise themselves. The squatters in Greer County did not stop to ask "under which king." They set up an organization and chose a county seat. Many of them being from Texas, and Texas being willing, they attached themselves for the time being to Texas.

This Greer County is an exceedingly well-favored country. It has as good soil as the Panhandle wheat belt, and it is better watered than some parts of the Panhandle. It has raised this year 2,000,000 bushels of wheat, and the three new mills and the three new elevators which form an impressive group at Quanah, in the Panhandle, are a tribute to Greer County's growing importance. Quanah is named for the Comanche chief, and with Vernon, shares the most of the Greer County trade. If the United States gets Greer the squatters will accommodate themselves to the homestead law and get 160 acres apiece. If Texas sustains her claim, the farmers contributing this crop of 2,000,000 bushels of wheat will be entitled to buy on the easy terms of the Texas land law 640 acres apiece. That is the reason the Panhandle towns hope the United States will win. They want a country of 160-acre farms right beside them to show how much better is the policy of small farms. And the most of the Panhandle lawyers say there is no doubt the United States will prove the South Fork is the main river and that Greer County is outside of Texas. To-day, where the Denver road crosses Red River, just beyond the corner of Greer, there is not a drop of water in sight—only an expanse of fiery red silt and sand half a mile wide between low banks. But a storm on the plains or in the mountains may send 7 feet of boiling red mud rolling down the channel in a few hours. So it depends on temporary circumstances which is Red River and which is the fork that doesn't count. A settlement of the boundary dispute will come before the end of the year it is thought. People who contribute 2,000,000 bushels of wheat to the visible supply must be given a political status. They may count in Oklahoma's early claim for statehood.

The traveler leaving Fort Worth for the Panhandle country rides almost due north for a couple of hours. He sees wheat fields stretching away in the distance. Great straw piles loom up like pyramids. The steam threshers toot a cheerful salute as the train rushes by. One of these threshers turned out 1611 bushels of wheat on Wednesday, and then broke its own record on Saturday with 1624 bushels. This kind of work was made possible by wheat giving twenty-five bushels to the acre. After the wheat fields come natural meadows, on which the baled hay is piled up as high as a horse and left almost wholly unprotected, with a firm faith in favoring weather. The meadows give place to pastures bounded only by the horizon. At Calef, fourteen miles north of Forth Worth, there are just five houses in sight on perhaps 10,000 acres of land. This is not the red lands or the Panhandle country. It is Tarrant County, of which Fort Worth is the seat. Tarrant County is where the idea of smaller farms and more people is being agitated with a great deal of vigor. Somebody asked Mr. Peter Smith, the ex-Mayor of Fort Worth, how much land a certain resident of the county had. "He hasn't much," Mr. Smith replied; "only about 1,000 acres." That illustrates the Texas idea of a small farm. Upon the public domain the United States considers 160 acres enough for a homestead. Texas kept all of her land when she became one of the States in 1846, and she gave it away or sold it in great blocks for many years. Having grown somewhat economical, Texas now sells only a section of agricultural land, or 640 acres, to one person—four times what the General Government allows. There is one man in Tarrant County who has 9,000 acres. He has fenced his farm, but he cultivates only 200 acres. There are others who haven't quite so much, but they have enough to make Tarrant County look like a grazing country, whereas "the fact is," said Gen. Clark, of Fort Worth, "we have as fine farming land as can be found anywhere."

The man with the 9,000 acres has declared his willingness to cut this farm up and sell it in alternate blocks. The Fort Worth Board of Trade is carrying on a campaign of education to make this change from pastures to farms general. According to the census figures Tarrant County has added only fifty-eight to her agricultural population in ten years. Fort Worth grew 16,413 in the decade, but the county outside of the city practically stood still. The people in the city have reached a

A GROUP OF COWBOYS.

logical conclusion that their future growth depends upon a change in the agricultural, or rather non-agricultural, conditions of the county. Hence the campaign. Like most other campaigns of education, this is not altogether encouraging. Texans let go of land, even when they are land-poor, with reluctance. A man who has 5,000 acres worth $12 now, and that is about the Tarrant County estimate of the big pastures; can hardly bring himself to sell 2,500 acres at $12, though it is made clear to him it will bring in people and make the remaining 2,500 worth $24.

THE LONE COURT HOUSE ON THE PRAIRIE.

The Panhandle, in spite of the progress of the man with the hoe, has the pasture problem to deal with. There isn't much doubt what the final result will be. Until he got the Cor... he out the cowman did not rest, and w... .ue same aggressive, not to say exterminating spirit, the farmer is now camping on the trail of the cowman. The famous red lands stretch from the Red River southwest. A tongue reaches the Concho. The main body extends on the northwest to Clarendon. But still farther into the Panhandle the man with the hoe has pushed his way. He may not find natural wheat country all over Northwestern Texas, but he has the faith of a pioneer that he can raise something.

The land which the cowman got at 50c and $1 is now worth from $6 to $10 an acre at a distance of five to seven miles from town. Within three and four miles of town it is worth $10 and $15 an acre. The State, at the instance of the cowman, classed it as grazing land. The man with a hoe, after five years' cropping says that 75 per cent of it is farming land and only 25 per cent pasture.

"This is land," said John Howard, of Wichita Falls, "which, with average seasons, will pay for itself, for the labor and for the seed in two years. That is something I don't believe can be done in any other State in the Union. What I've done others will do. I've given an Iowa man a three years' lease on some land of mine. He fences, improves and has all he can raise for three years. At the end of that time the fencing is mine. If he puts up a house I pay him for that. With the kind of crops we have had for five years that man will make enough to pay him for his labor and to buy him some land at the end of the three years. This plan gives a man from the North a chance to try the country and see if he likes it. Texans won't take the land on such terms, but Northern men will. The latter don't like to go in debt and are timid about settling here permanently without a trial. By giving the entire use of the land for that term of years we interest a tenant in cultivating it well."

It isn't much wonder that Northern men hesitate to take the Panhandle on faith. A few years ago the banner wheat county of this region was known far and wide as "Wicked Wilbarger." Civilization goes with wheat. Judge Orr and some associates went down to Austin and persuaded the State authorities that Wilbarger should be classed as agricultural lands. Two or three other counties in the Panhandle were equally successful. The result was the selling of their lands in single sections, thicker settlement, more wheat and less wickedness. It was 'Wicked Wilbarger" showed 55.28 per cent, increase of population by the new census. Adjoining counties of the same kind of land were not so fortunate. At Austin the cowmen were too quick for the man with the hoe; the land was classed as grazing and sold in blocks of seven sections. There the fight against the pastures is still on.

W. B. S.

THROUGH TEXAS.

The First Round-Up for Law and Order in the Panhandle.

A Hundred Killings—Tascosa's Grand Jury—Memories of Boot Hill—The Great X. I. T.—Pasture Disintegration.

Special correspondence of the Globe-Democrat.

IN THE PANHANDLE OF TEXAS, August 7.— There hasn't been an interment on Boot Hill for more than two years. Things have changed since Henry King died. Tascosa, once "the toughest town" of the Panhandle, has a big new Court House. If the ghost of Billy the Kid could come back it would find but one familiar Landmark—Boot Hill. The Denver train steams into and out of Tascosa about the hour that graveyards yawn. Not a single pistol shot disturbs the slumbers of the passengers.

came to Tascosa a hundred miles and more to get supplies. And they didn't leave without having had what they called "a wide time." Tascosa was the meeting point where troubles were settled long before a stone court house with a cupola was thought of. The feuds of the ranches, the disputes between cowboys and gamblers, the rivalries over favors of frail creatures, all came to an issue at Tascosa. And when the arbitrament of navy sixes had been pronounced there was an addition to be made to the population of Boot Hill. The pessimists say that epitaphs lie. The records on the head boards of Boot Hill faithfully record history. Boot Hill is a sightly knoll a little way out of Tascosa. Only those who died with their boots on were entitled to a place on the hill. Life was too practical in the Panhandle to encourage the erection of elaborate monuments. A board was deemed sufficiently permanent. On it was inscribed enough to remind the friends and to warn the enemies of the deceased. Many of the boards have fallen down or have disappeared. Perhaps they lasted long enough to serve their double purpose.

Perhaps it was grand juries and courts. More likely it was wheat-raising and the man with the hoe which wrought the revolution in the value of human life. But to-day no man need carry a gun on his hip in the Panhandle. There is a detachment of rangers

A WICHITA FALLS MELON FIELD.

Tascosa, Mexican by name and American by adoption, is one of the oldest settlements in the Panhandle. For years it was the outfitting post of a great cow country. Ranchers

up here. The officer in command is Lieut. Britton.

"We haven't much to do now," the Lieutenant said, as he leaned on the gate of the corral, "beyond helping the Sheriff to overtake fugitives from justice. We make scouts cover the country to see what is going on and occasionally we are called on to run down a murder. But the work is nothing like what it was a few years ago. There is no train robbing. We haven't had a case of shooting out the lights in a long time. Now and then a cowboy comes to town and gets full. Perhaps he will begin to make a noise. We go to him and take him by the arm and tell him it won't do. He usually quiets down and that is all there is of it."

There is still some big ranching in the Panhandle. From the northern boundary of the State one fence extends 210 miles due south. This isn't as great as the distance from St. Louis to Chicago, but it is a good part of it. This single fence belongs to one company. It bounds the east line of the possessions of the X. I. T. There is another fence on the west side, and there are cross fences dividing this, the largest fenced pasture in the world, into divisions. On each division is a big house, a superintendent and a force of men. It requires 125 men to run this ranch. The smallest of the pasture divisions contains 470,000 acres. Last year 50,000 calves were branded on this ranch. Yet the chief owner in this magnificent property "wishes he had never seen a cow brute." His name is Farwell, and he is a merchant prince in Chicago. Years ago, when Texas had more land than anything else, she proclaimed through the newspapers that she would give so many million acres of land for a State Capitol so big. It was a novel proposition. Takers were found in the Farwells, of Chicago; Abner Taylor the present Congressman, and his father-in-law, Mr. Babcock, an Illinois banker. These gentlemen built a Capitol of the length, breadth and height specified in the bond, and they got their pay in this Panhandle pasture, 210 miles long. Texas lands went up and down and up again while the Capitol was building. The then unfenced and unstocked pasture was worth at one time twice what the Capitol cost. It was worth at another time, when the bottom fell out of the cattle business, less than the Capitol cost. It would sell now for enough to build half a dozen capitols.

The "nester" has not yet tackled the Capitol syndicate land, but there is hardly a Texas pasture east of the 210 miles fence in which farmers have not found foothold. Cowmen can acquire great blocks of land, but they often have to inclose with their purchases the school sections, for the use of which they pay rental. The nester comes along, and begins farming on one of the school sections. Whenever the school section is wanted for agricultural purposes the cowman's lease expires. For the nester's accommodation the pasture owner must put in gates and allow roadways. This is one way in which the disintegration of the large pastures begins. Texas has had a land policy full of inconsistencies. Some of these results may be seen in a ride through the Panhandle. For example, between Vernon and Wichita Falls the wheat fields extend on either side of the Denver road as far as the vision reaches. East of Wichita Falls the right of way is bounded by wire fences, and beyond is the virgin prairie, with here and there a fresh breaking or a new house. The difference is that in one case the farmer got in his work at Austin, and in the other the cowman had the ear of the Administration. In one case the county was classed as agricultural. In the other, although the land was of precisely the same character, the decision was "grazing." One man could buy a single section only of agricultural land. He could obtain seven sections of grazing. And so one county was turned into wheat fields and another into pastures. East of Wichita Falls the railroad runs through a pasture of 17,000 acres good for twenty-four bushels of wheat in the average season. This pasture might, for all of the purposes of town growth and railroad traffic, have been a desert. But it has passed into the hands of a Nebraska man and an Iowa man, and they are turning it into farms at $8 and $10 an acre. North of Wichita Falls and Iowa Park lies a barrier in the form of a pasture of 25,000 acres. This pasture comes down to within three miles of the Falls. It belongs to Dan Waggoner and Burke Burnett, the cattle kings. Burnett's home is in Fort Worth. Waggoner has a fine stone mansion prettily located on an elevation above the railroad at Decatur. The people of Wichita Falls and Iowa Park are grumbling mightily. "Of what use is it," they say, "to ship four car loads of melons a day or to grind nearly 1,000 barrels of flour every twenty-four hours if progress is to be barred by such a barrier?" Beyond the pasture lies that part of the Indian Territory known as the Fort Sill country, the home of the Comanches. Envious eyes are upon the Waggoner pasture and upon the Fort Sill country, "Take the farmers out of this region," say the Iowa Park people, "and property wouldn't be worth 10c on the dollar. Double the number of farmers and property will be worth 150c on the dollar of the present valuation. The way to boom the town is to say nothing about it but to settle the farms."

There is room in the Waggoner pasture for 500 farmers. People would pay $10 to $15 an acre for the land if they could get it. Before the country, in other directions from Wichita Falls, was developed, the Waggoner pasture wasn't worth over $3 or $4 an acre. The settlement of the Waggoner pasture would double the population of Iowa Park in two years. Thus the issue of anti-pasture grows in the Panhandle. The Waggoner pasture is mentioned only as an illustration. All through the Panhandle this issue exists. It is greater than any other question. County elections turn upon it. Until three years ago the cowmen controlled the Panhandle politics. They elected County Commissioners and dictated assessment and taxation. They let the farmers' improvements bear the burden, while the big pastures which were increased in value by such improvements beside them were taxed only as wild land. The opening of roads was retarded. The contest was and is a lively one. Self-interest of the cowmen is arrayed against self-interest of the farmers. Neither is blame-worthy. A few years ago twenty men named the officers and shaped the policies of four of these wheat-growing counties. But big pastures don't go with big towns. And this is the era of farm-making and town-building in the Panhandle.

Who would have dreamed that the cowman and Comanche would ever lie down together? The cowman dispossessed the Comanche. He drove him from the Panhandle into a reservation. And now the Comanche is in the pay of the cowman to help stay the progress of the farmer. The Fort Sill country is so near that the Comanches trot their ponies down to Wichita Falls in a day. It is the cream of the Indian Territory in the opinion of the Panhandle farmer. But while other reservations in the Territory are being broken up and thrown open to white settlement, the Fort Sill country remains closed. The big man among the Comanches is Quanah Porter. Quanah has a farm and plenty of horses. He has taken sides with the cowman, his old enemy. When it is necessary to send a squad of Comanche chiefs to Washington to tell the Great Father the Comanches want to lease their lands to Dan Waggoner and the other cattle kings for 6c a year per acre, Quanah is the shrewd Comanche who rounds up the squad and has charge of them. Quanah is a politician. He is not much of a chief by inheritance or by war-path record. But he is a very smart Indian politician. When Mackenzie killed 3600 Indian ponies down at the mouth of the Tule and hustled the Comanches back on their reservation after their last breakaway he picked out Quanah and put him at the head of the whole outfit. By virtue of this commission from the great "long gun," and by the exercise of a good deal of practical politics, Quanah has remained boss of the Comanches to this day. Something happened not long ago which nearly ended Quanah's usefulness with his people. The boss gathered together a lot of big men of the tribe and took them down to Fort Worth on a junket. The cowmen wanted a job put through, it matters little what. The Comanches were corraled in the best hotel in the fort. The next morning one of them was dead. He had blown out the gas. The chief's body was taken back to the Fort Sill country. There was great lamentation. Many ponies were killed for use in the happy hunting grounds. Braves gashed their breasts and squaws howled. Suspicion of foul play fell upon Quanah, and in the excitement of grief there was strong sentiment in favor of sending Quanah to join the departed. But his white friends stood by the boss. Time effaced the memory of the affliction. To-day Quanah is more a boss than ever, and he stands in with the cowmen to their great satisfaction and his own material

FORMER OWNERS OF THE PANHANDLE.

benefit. The Panhandle farmers say there is room for 50,000 people, without crowding, in the Fort Sill country. They say that if the title to Greer is vested in the United States, that new country bordering the Comanches reservation on the west will have 100,000 people in ninety days. And they also say that the United States land policy of 160 acres, enough for a homestead, would put 10,000,000 in Texas by the time the population of the whole country reaches 100,000,000. Perhaps they are right. Oklahoma was settled in a day. The Cheyenne and Arapahoe lands were filed on in another day. South of them lie the Fort Sill country, Greer County and the Panhandle. Southwestward the star of empire takes its way.   W. B. S.

THROUGH TEXAS.

Strange Sights and Stranger Tales of the Transpecos Country.

A Monument Not Made with Hands—The Mystery of Diablo Canyon—Mountain Kangaroo—The Ancient Irrigators

Special Correspondence of the Globe-Democrat.

SIERRA BLANCA, TEX., August 13.—After the tireless American tourist has exhausted the rest of the continent, he can come to the transpecos country and find brand new wonders. Beyond the Pecos River lies a part of Texas as large as all New England, leaving off Maine. It has more mountains than people, and it is full of strange things. Five or six miles north of the little station of Van Horn is something worth coming miles to see. A ledge of blood-red sandstone overhangs the ravine. It projects outward from 50 to 150 feet and is from 100 to 200 feet above the bottom. Under this massive roof one can walk for five or six miles. An army could be sheltered there. At the upper end of this almost enclosed ravine rises a natural monument. It is of rock, built up strata upon strata to the enormous height of 300 feet. That is more than half of the height of the Washington Monument. This strange freak looks like an old tower. The stratification gives it all of the appearance of rock laid course upon course by human hands. The base is 100 feet square and the top tapers to about 50 feet. Some day there will be pictures of this monument in the guide books, and people will travel the 740 miles from East Texas to West Texas to see it and other works of nature in the transpecos country.

At a somewhat greater distance from the railroad is the Diablo Canyon. The Pueblo shrugs his shoulders when he talks of the Diablo Canyon. It is in the wildest and ruggedest parts of the mountains. More antelope can be seen in the canyon than anywhere else in the country. There are literally thousands of them. This is because all life in the Diablo Canyon is sacred to the Indians, and white men almost never penetrate the mysterious precincts. These antelope have not been disturbed. Anywhere outside of the canyon the antelope is the Indian's meat. Within the canyon sanctity permits no killing. As a rule the Indians do not visit the place. But in the tribe are several who seem to have been initiated into an order or mystic body. These

THE CACTUS GARDEN AT SIERRA BLANCA.

have the right of entering the canyon. They exercise a kind of guardianship over it. White men do not visit the Diablo Canyon because they can find no water in or near it. Yet there is water. Springs abound, and the location of them is a secret the Indian holds. The water from these springs runs a short distance and then sinks into the ground. That is a great trick with the water courses throughout this region. White men and all but the initiated, may pass within a few feet of one of these springs and never suspect its presence. The water is covered entirely over from its source to its place of disappearance in the earth with dry hides. Upon the hides dirt has been scattered and grass sown. This work was done long ago by the initiated to preserve the sacredness of the canyon, and it has proven effective. The initiated members of the tribe can go to these springs. None others can find one of them. The Diablo Canyon is seven or eight miles long, surrounded by precipices and reached only by difficult trails. It is thirty miles from the railroad.

IN THE GUADALUPE MOUNTAINS.

There are nuts and grains in the transpecos mountains. White men have never found them. The Indians can go to them at any time and can obtain subsistence where white men would starve. Cactus growth takes on its most fantastic forms in this region. There are cactus trees and cactus shrubs and cactus plants. At a little distance some of these collections look like well-kept gardens. The cactus seems to have been set out by human design in regular rows and squares. But a nearer view shows that nature's orderly inspiration has done it all. At the station of Sierra Blanca specimens of the different varieties of cactus growth have been brought from the mountain sides and grouped. They are not only of all forms and sizes, but of many colors, and alike only in the possession of the sharp needles.

There is something besides mountain and cactus in the transpecos country. Coming out of the Davis mountains is Toyah Creek. It is a sparkling mountain stream, 15 to 20 feet in width in places, making a succession on rheumatism and gout, and have wrought cures. The elevation is high. The climate is dry. It tones up weak lungs and enables the asthmatic to whoop and enjoy life. Here are salt-water bathing and mountain air combined. Yet the man who wishes to enjoy the combination must sleep out of doors or take a tent along. There are no accommodations. Nature has created an extraordinary variety of conditions for a great sanitarium and pleasure resort, but no one has had the enterprise to build a hotel. This Toyah Creek and the lake are only a dozen miles south of Pecos City. They are to-day just as nature made them, save for the partial use of the creek water for irrigating.

The transpecos country has its living as well as its inanimate freaks. Upon the large

THE CARRIZO MOUNTAINS, NORTH OF VAN HORN.

of deep pools and dashing over falls until it reaches the more level country. There it forms a beautiful lake two miles wide and four miles in length. On the creek are half a dozen irrigating canals taking out water to irrigate from 5,000 to 10,000 acres of land. This creek is full of fish, including what is called trout in this country, but what is not like any trout in Northern mountain streams. In season the creek and lake are covered with game ducks and other water fowl of every description. The lake is salt, in spite of the mountain feeder. It has a smooth beach and a hard bottom. It is free from holes and is a most perfect bathing place. There are springs all about which possess a whole apothecary shop of medical qualities. Some of these springs have been tested table in the room, at Dallas, where the Texas and Pacific World's Fair exhibit is being prepared, two curious animals have their temporary home. They are "most amoosin little cusses." In the transpecos country, from which these animals were sent a few days ago to Mr. Roessler, they are known as mountain kangaroos. There are others where these came from, but the man who catches them will have to be quicker than the Irishman was with the flea. The name is well bestowed. They are kangaroos, but of liliputian mold. Their bodies are about 4 inches long, with reddish brown fur on the back and the most delicate white fur on the belly. They have hind legs 7 inches long, nearly twice the length of the body. The front legs are about one inch long. The tail is 7 inches long, and has quite a bushy covering at the end. On the tail and the hind legs these little kangaroos sit, and use the fore legs for hands. Their movement is by jumps, and they go like lightning. All that one sees is a red streak. Strange to tell, the little fellows take to tameness and civilization very kindly. They are rarely caught, owing to their ability to get away. But once caged they become domesticated in a few hours. All that they want to make them perfectly happy is something to do. And therein they set a fine example for Texas politicians. Mr. Roessler puts a pint of grain at one end of the large table and a large paper funnel at the other. In half an hour the two kangaroos will move the heap of seed across the table and store it in the paper funnel. As they squat beside the grain they seem to be eating it, but instead of pouring it into their mouths with their paws they tuck it away in two pouches, one on either side of the head, and when loaded they jump across the table at a pace which would have turned Mark Twain's frog green with envy, and unload it in the hiding place. As often as the grain heap is replenished these indefatigable workers will remove it to the improvised store house.

These mountain kangaroos of West Texas live in the dryest places and altitudes of from 3000 to 5000 feet. They make their nests or homes on the ground, usually about the roots of a tree. They use sticks and put them together so nicely as to make a solid little structure. Mr. Roessler has searched the books and found no description of his new pets. That in natural history which most resembles the little kangaroo of the transpecos is the jerboa of Africa.

The Pecos valley is being bored full of artesian wells and gridironed with irrigation systems. Half a dozen years ago this was the Death's Valley of the cattle drive. The cowboys knew it to their sorrow. Coming up from South Texas with their yearlings and 2-year-olds bound for the ranges of Colorado, Wyoming and Montana, the cattlemen were forced to follow the Pecos River. There was no other route. The only water was in the river and the grass for a long way on either side was trampled out or gnawed to the roots. So the herds zigzagged up the valley, drifting off as far as they dared to go without water for feed, and then angling back to the river, in an almost parched condition.

"I remember it well," said one of these same cattlemen, who is now selling town lots and improved farms at Eddy. "In 1886 our outfit tried to drive out of Texas by this route to Montana. We never had such a time in our lives. We lost between 500 and 600 head. It was leave the river and drive to the hills for feed; then leave the hills and drive to the river for water. Other outfits fared worse than we did, getting through with losses of 5000 and 6000. The valley was strewn with dead s ck."

Lebold the transformation. All of the way up the valley from Pecos City in Texas to Roswell in New Mexico not 100 people were living. And now the Pecos Valley is well on the way to achieve a population of 200,000 or 300,000 inhabitants. Irrigation is doing it. Perhaps, after all, this isn't so wonderful. When the pioneer surveying party went over that part of the valley near Delaware Creek, running the lines for a big canal, they found the ground plan of an ancient city. The streets were laid with cobble stones, and are there to-day. They are extensive enough to show that a large community must have been served by them. The adobe houses which

EXTINCT GEYSER IN PECOS VALLEY.

lined these streets have melted away under the storms of perhaps half a dozen centuries, but no one who walks the streets can doubt that the populous city once existed. This ancient site is some miles north of Pecos City. Forty miles south of Pecos City another party of surveyors came upon an ancient canal. That canal is now in use as part of a system. Mr. O. W. Williams says the lines of the ancient canal are as accurate as any engineer could make them to-day. The ancient city and the ancient canal tell the story. Hundreds of years ago, before Columbus came, this Pecos Valley was settled and irrigated by people who lived in cities and knew how to run levels. History is only repeating itself on a grander and a modern scale along the Pecos.

Up and down the Pecos Valley are mounds. If the few inches of soil is scraped off there is uncovered a mass of broken rock and black ashes. The rock is reduced to about the size of macadam. It looks as if it had gone through a mighty crusher. Some of this broken rock is granite. There is no other granite found on the surface for hundreds of miles around. Some of the fragments are lava. The ashes are like the scoriæ of volcanic action. The centers of the mounds are hollow. At the rising town of Eddy the enterprising people have made streets of the contents of these mounds, and though they have dug down considerable distances they have found the same curious mixture of broken rock and ashes as far as they have gone. The local theory is that each of these mounds is an extinct geyser. Mr. G. O. Shields, of Eddy, has made something of a study of the mounds. He says "the country is full of them." They are found along the Pecos and up its tributaries. Mr. Shields says that they bear every appearance of having been active within a comparatively recent period, perhaps not longer than a century. It may be there are geysers still spouting in the mountains and that may explain the mystery of the Diablo Canyon, which all Indians venerate as the abode of spirits. W. B. S.

THROUGH TEXAS.

An Ancient People Whose City Was Built When Columbus Came.

The Story of the Tihuas—Their Glorious Deeds in War—A Sacred Tradition Which Was Not A Secret— Mining in West Texas.

Special Correspondence of the Globe-Democrat.

YSLETA, TEX., August 14.—This nation is about to celebrate "The Discovery of America." Yet it has voters to whom the coming of Columbus was only an incident. Before the Spanish conquest Ysleta was a city. The Ysleta people had their politics, their history, their government, their statesmen and their generals. It is much more than 400 years next October since they took up their residence on the border of the Rio Grande in Texas. The community has its leading citizens and they talk freely and interestingly. They say that originally they came from the Colorado River of the West. Two branches of quite a nation moved eastward at the same time to find new homes. One settled at Ysleta, in what is now Texas; the other at Ysleta, in the present New Mexico. They had government and they built cities. The Texas Ysleta prospered best. Apaches and Comanches viewed the new-comers as intruders and tried to drive them back. They besieged the upper colony, and Ysleta in Texas was obliged to send a military force to help out the brethren. That force remained, and the descendants are still living in the Ysleta of New Mexico. These people are now called Pueblos. Their distinctive name as a tribe or nation was Tihua. Ysleta was originally Chihua. For 100 years war was waged against the Indians who sought to drive back the Tihuas. Then the Spaniards came in and overran the country. The Tihuas accepted the conquest. But submission was not because of superior military prowess. It was for a religious reason. For a time the relations ran smoothly. The Spaniards mistook the nature of this people. They thought they were too tame to fight, and they became oppressive. The Tihuas arose in revolution and drove the Spaniards out of New Mexico and Texas. After that for a hundred years there was war between the Tihuas and the Spaniards. The latter, with better armament and with increased forces, gradually worsted the

THE CHISAS MOUNTAINS, TEXAS.

former. But this time there was no submission. The Tihuas fighting stubbornly withdrew from their ancient city of Chihua, gave up their fields and vineyards and their elaborate irrigation system and moved eastward,

A HOME OF THE TIHUAS.

even across the Pecos River. They built new towns, and made a stronghold in the Hueco mountains. Hueco has been Americanized into Waco. In Hueco Mountains the last battle with the Spaniards was fought. And when the so-called "conquerors" tired of trying to subdue the Tihuas the latter, many of them, have given the United States soldiers by their wily ways and desperate tactics this victory of the Tihuas appears the more remarkable. According to the story told at Ysleta by the local chroniclers of the Tihuas, the Apaches surprised and murdered two of the Pueblos at what is now Carrizo Station, on the Texas and Pacific Railroad. The Tihuas mustered their fighting strength and their best officers took the field. By a series of forced marches and by brilliant maneuvers they drove the Apaches, between 300 and 400 strong, into the Hueco Mountains, and finally into a great cavern. There they penned them in. Sixty of the Apaches died of starvation. In a series of desperate sorties 75 per cent were killed. Enough got away to carry the news to the tribe. In the language again of the interpreter: "The Apaches never monkeyed with the Tihuas after that."

These Pueblos have been given the reputation of being patient and peace-loving by the historians and ethnologists. They have been credited with being submissive almost to the degree of accepting tyranny in preference to strife. It would appear that this trait has

A VEHICLE AND GRANARY IN ANCIENT YSLETA.

moved back to their beloved Ysleta, repaired the ditches and remade the city. This is history, not as will be found in the books, but as it is told to-day by the best men of Ysleta, than whom the United States has no better assimilated citizens. Until twenty years ago the Tihuas fought the Apaches, their hereditary enemies. Peace was established as the result of a brilliant campaign. In the language of the interpreter, the Tihuas "did them up in great shape." When it is remembered how much trouble the Apaches been overdrawn. Army officers say that the Tihuas will fight. They have tried them as trailers and scouts in the Indian campaigns and have found them full of strategy and grit. Next to the Apaches the Comanches ranked in savage valor. Yet the Tihuas forced an understanding with the Comanches and established a boundary which neither crossed. After the Hueco tragedy the same kind of a treaty was made with the Apaches.

The cave in which the Apaches perished is treated to this day as a place to be avoided. No Indian will enter it. They say the spirits of the starved and slaughtered Apaches still linger there. The visitor can hear in one corner three distinct raps. They seem to come from another part of the cave. When the sound is followed to what seems to be the source it is heard again, but coming fro a somewhere else. These three raps can be heard at intervals. Sometimes they seem to come from above and sometimes from below. They are such raps as might be made by striking the rock sharply with a hammer. After the raps comes a whistling or hissing sound. Nobody has ever been able to account for the rappings. All Indians of whatever tribe give the cave a wide berth. The location of this mystery is northeast of El Paso about twenty-five miles.

closely resemble the doctrines of the Christian religion. Cuetzalcoatl taught the art of working silver. He educated the Aztecs in agriculture, trained them in the weaving of cloth, gave them forms of worship, and inculcated the idea of making sacrifices only of flowers. And when the god had thus finished his work he sailed eastward on a raft of snakes, promising to return some time. When the Spaniards landed, their cross-emblazoned banners, their religious customs and their manners brought back the memory of the god of air. The natives were sure that Cuetzalcoatl had come again. They made haste to welcome. They submitted to Spanish domination until it grew tyrannical. Cortez got in his cruel work before the mistake was discovered.

AN ANCIENT PEAR TREE AT YSLETA.

And now for the explanation of the submission of these people to the Spaniards, an act on which is based misapprehension of their character. Not long ago a gentleman familiar with Aztec lore visited Ysleta in Texas. He brought together the chief men of the Tihuas and made them a speech. In the course of the remarks, which were interpreted sentence by sentence, the visitor told the legend of Cuetzalcoatl. The purpose was to judge of the effect of the narrative upon the Tihuas and to determine their possible relationship to the Aztecs. Cuetzalcoatl was the Aztec god of air. His functions were those of a priest. Many of his teachings, as described by the Aztecs,

Thus the story of Cuetzalcoatl was narrated to the Tihuas of Western Texas for the first time by a white man. In the audience were men of great age. Their excitement increased as the narrative progressed. As soon as the end was reached there was a commotion. The listeners looked at each other and then at the speaker. They conversed together in an excited manner. They turned to the interpreter and wanted to know where the white man had learned what he had told. Then they said that the story of Cuetzalcoatl was one of their most sacred memories, and they did not dream it was known to any but themselves. Finding that he knew so much, the Tihuas told many things going to show their common origin with the Aztecs of Mexico and Yucatan. They told of the sacred fires which had been burning centuries for the return of the god. They confirmed the theory that it was the belief in the return of Cuetzalcoatl which had prompted their submission to the Spanish yoke.

These Tihuas pay taxes and vote; they fulfil all of the duties and exercise all of the privileges of American citizens. At the same time they preserve the old forms and offices of Aztec self-government. But the latter is now social rather than political. The Aztec government is a reminiscence. The real government is American.

Perhaps the Tihuas are the original longhorns. "X" is interchangeable with "hu" in the ancient spelling and pronunciation. With this borne in mind it is not difficult to see a close relationship between Tihuas, pronounced Te-waus, and Texas. The derivation of Texas has given the scholars of the Southwest a great deal of trouble. The history of the Tihuas may have a bearing on the controversy.

These mountains of Texas look as if they ought to contain rich ores. In their continuation to the northward are prosperous mining camps. To the south are located some of the famous mines of Mexico. Yet up to date, Texas as a mining country for the precious metals, is almost a terra incognita. There has been some prospecting, and there is some mining going on in Western Texas. There may be a great deal more. North of El Paso is the Franklin district. Fifteen miles southwest of Sierra Blanca, where the cactus gardens cover the mountain side, is a second district. The Carrizo mines are six miles from Allamore Station. There is a district called the Diabolo north of Van Horn. Precious minerals are also found in the mountains 150 to 200 miles south of Pecos City. The Frank-

ON THE PLATFORM AT WILD HORSE, TEX.

lin district has been prospected in a small way. Very little has been done in development. In the Carrizo district the ores which have been found are usually green copper, with silver varying from $30 to $150 a ton.

THE CHURCH AT YSLETA, THREE HUNDRED YEARS OLD.

In this district there are numerous prospect holes, but no mines in operation. The Diabolo Mountains are the palisades of Texas. Seen from the car window the palisades appear to be about 150 feet high. But at a distance from the railroad these palisades tower magnificently to the height of 1,000 and 1,500 feet above the surrounding country. In the Diabolo Mountains the Hazel mines are situated. They are worked by 200 men, and quite a little town has come into existence eight miles from Allamore Station. The ore is what is known as tetrahedrite, or gray copper. It carries from 100 to 1,600 ounces of silver to the ton. Much of the silver found is wire. The percentage of copper is about 20. There are any number of prospect holes in the district around the Hazel mines. Southwest of Sierra Blanca the trail winds its way through the natural cactus gardens to the Bonanza mines. The product is a combination of silver and lead. It is 35 to 40 per cent lead, and furnishes from 40 to 150 ounces of silver to the ton. This district is within six miles of Etholen Station. It is worked only in a small way.

In Presidio County, a long distance south of the districts just mentioned, are located the Presidio and Cibolo mines at Shafter. They have been worked for several years. The ores are galena, sulphurets and chlorides of silver mixed more or less with iron. They give 200 to 500 ounces of silver to the ton and are accounted very valuable mines.

Ores have been found in many places in the mountains of Western Texas, but the mining industry is in its infancy. W. B. S.

THROUGH TEXAS.

The Story of Three Men and Their Three Millions Investment.

Where Jay Gould Found Health and a Railroad—Holy River—Irrigation Made Easy for Beginners—A Woman's Expensive Desert Land Entry.

Special Correspondence of the Globe Democrat.

IN THE PECOS VALLEY, August 15.—Two years ago there was a piece of land 400 miles square without a rod of railroad. From the center it was possible to journey 200 miles in any direction and not read "Look out for the locomotive." Nowhere else in the United States was this true. One man had a ranch house here. His cattle roamed over several thousand hills and yielded little profit. Another man came. He had made a snug fortune as superintendent of iron works at Milwaukee, had swelled it by fortunate investment in iron lands in the Lake Superior region; still further increased it by the building of a Colorado railroad, and was receiving $1000 a month from his interest in a single Colorado mine. The third man was a newspaper editor and publisher. He had lived fifteen years on hope in this region. His sole capital was experience. These three men pooled their brains, their capital and their experience. They acquired the land. They made a whole river their servant, taking every drop of water out of the channel. They built a railroad a hundred miles long. Around a $50,000 hotel and a $30,000 court house they laid out a city. "The timidity of capital" is talked about. The proposition which these three men laid before the world has absorbed $3,000,000. And the ditching and planting and building go on with supreme faith in the ultimate result.

This Pecos Valley enterprise is a part of "Through Texas," although the lands and the headquarters of the grand scheme lie in the southeastern corner of New Mexico. Far up in the mountains of New Mexico the Rio Pecos has its rise. It crosses the line into Texas near the corner of the Territory and continues on its course through Western Texas to its junction with the Rio Grande. At the crossing of the Texas and Pacific Railroad and the Rio Pecos, the new railroad of the Pecos Valley has its connection with the world. It comes down the Pecos Valley from Eddy, in New Mexico, a distance of ninety miles.

The soil of the Pecos Valley is dark, with some gravel here, some gypsum there and occasional alkali beds. It is the same soil which in the Rio Grande and other arid valleys looks hopeless until water is turned upon it, and then, behold! It becomes Paradise. When the three men began the grand work of transformation in the Pecos Valley this land was rated by the Government at $1.25 an acre, and there were no takers. A dam was built over the river from side to side, to catch the entire flow. It is 50 feet high and 1150 feet long. Just above the shrewdly chosen location the river comes down and strikes with its full force a high limestone bluff. It turns sharply and meets the dam with the current almost destroyed by the bluff. Around the end of the dam, hewn out of this solid limestone bluff, 30 feet wide and 25 feet deep, is the channel through which the water is led off into the great irrigating canal. Heavy gates set into the rock bottom and sides control the water as perfectly as if this was the lock of a canal. The lake made by the dam is seven miles long and two miles wide, holding in reserve 1,000,000,000 gallons of water. There is the inspiration of the 100 miles of railroad, the large hotel, the town, the land which nobody would take at $1 25 now worth all of the way from $5 to $50 an acre—in short of the whole $3,000,000 investment.

But the $3,000,000 doesn't represent the end. The plans of the founders of this ambitious city and irrigation scheme contemplate the expenditure of $2,000,000 before they are anywhere near complete. After that it is expected the enterprise will carry itself.

The water in the canal flows gently with a fall of 18 inches to the mile. In the river channel the fall is 18 to 20 feet to the mile. It doesn't take very far to carry the water back from the river so that the whole valley's width, a dozen miles or more, is under the water level. The water coming down the headway hewn in the solid rock rushes through a dozen narrow gates into the canal. The engineers say that in each gate can be placed a turbine wheel which will develop 1000 horse-power. The power can be carried by wire down the valley and will supply a city of 50,000 people with all they need for light manufacturing. In this water to be supplied for irrigation is carried a red rich silt which will fertilize wherever the water moistens. This silt is equal to the best manure, and in twenty-five or thirty years will give the whole valley another top soil. Another dam twenty miles further up the river is included in the plan of further improvement. This will give a reservoir eight times as large as the present one. The Pecos is a queer river. Every drop in the channel is cut off by the dam. Yet half a mile below there is a running stream, and six miles below the dam the river is booming along merrily. It is replenished by enormous springs which boil up from the bed and sides. One of these streams pours out a volume of water greater than the City of Denver uses in twenty-four hours.

The canal is 45 feet wide at the bottom, and carries 7 feet of water. It is as large as the canals used for transportation purposes in the eastern part of the United States. Four miles below the dam the canal divides, the larger branch crosses the river it has just robbed on a monster flume 40 feet above the river bed, and continues down the valley sixty miles or more. The larger canals in the system now have a total length of over 100 miles, and the branches have as much more. The digging still goes on.

Mr. Gould came up the Pecos Valley awhile ago. He saw the dam, the town, the canals and the brand new farms. As he went about he asked so many questions that the representative of the company was almost floored. Before he left the valley Mr. Gould made Mr. Hagerman, one of "the big three" an offer for the railroad. Mr. Hagerman replied, "It is not for sale at any price, Mr. Gould." Before he moved on his special car in search of health and more railroads the magnate put on a piece of paper his opinion to this effect:

"I am impressed with the wonderful richness of the soil, with its peculiar adaptation to irrigation. With an ample supply of water it will not be long before it becomes one of the richest valleys in the United States. What I was particularly interested in is the effect of the pure, dry air on bronchial troubles. Speaking from personal experience,

THE BIG FLUME ACROSS THE PECOS.

there is no better region than this for persons thus suffering. The effect is immediate and improvement rapid."

The streets of Eddy are full of people who have come to the Pecos to prolong life. This is a climate so dry that to die means to dry up, not to decay. Delicate lunged men whose days were numbered in the North are down here selling goods, practicing the professions and making farms. With one lung, with even a piece of a lung, if it is not too small, one may enjoy life, liberty and the pursuit of happiness in the Pecos Valley. It is a novel community. Some men have come to save themselves. Other men have come to save their wives. Parents whose little flocks have begun to dwindle in the ruthless North have brought what they have left in the hope that the dreaded disease may not claim all.

In and about Eddy are a former railroad builder from Chicago, a retired army officer, two doctors from Fort Wayne, Ind., a retired merchant from La Crosse, Wis., another doctor from Van Wert, O., an Oakland (Ill.) merchant, a nephew of the late William H. Seward, Lincoln's Secretary of State, an Englishman and a Scotchman of means, a New Yorker, a civil engineer from St. Louis and a real estate man from the same place.

As evidence of the remarkable dryness of the climate, it is told a quarter of beef may be hung up out of doors. The surface will crust and the meat will be fresh until eaten.

But it isn't true that everybody in the Pecos Valley has come for health. Occasionally there is a man who has found this a place to make money. One such drew $25,000 in a lottery. He invested in a stock of lumber. Last year he cleared up $25,000, and this year he says he will make $50,000.

Irrigation is an art. It is something more than turning water upon land. The Pecos Valley presents at least one striking proof of this. A year ago a colony of Swiss was brought over and settled some miles south of Eddy. They had means. Some of them were sons of well-to-do families; they were given this start in life in a new country in the hope that they would do better than they had done in the old. When they came these Swiss were very fresh. They unbuckled every strap from bit to crupper when they unharnessed their horses. They managed to stir the soil, sowed their grain, let the water loose, and then sat down on the shady side of the houses to drink bottled beer and wait for the harvest. To-day the station of Vaud, named after a province of Switzerland, stands in the midst of a waste of drowned-out crops. The newcomer, entering the Pecos Eden by way of Vaud, wonders if this is what he came to see. Faith is only restored by a visit to the Greene vineyards, where 95 per cent of the nearly 250,000 grapevines planted on 520 acres of new land last February and March are alive and doing well. Three car loads of these rooted cuttings Mr. Greene bought at $18 a thousand and set out. To be exact, tho total number of settings was 212,500. Too much water is the danger in irrigation. The great vineyard has been irrigated only twice this season, but the stirring cultivators are going continuously. Many of these little vines, scarcely more than a finger's length when set out in March, have bunches of grapes this year.

Mr. Greene is one of the big three founders of the Eddy enterprise. He was a newspaper man at El Paso when he became interested here. His little paper was struggling. The editor was making a study of irrigation. The more he studied irrigation the greater grew his faith in it and the less he cared for his advertising columns. He visited the Pecos Valley in his pursuit of irrigation experience, and linked his fortunes with Mr. Eddy, the ranchman, and Mr. Hagerman, the railroad builder. Of the three Mr. Greene was the one who could talk. It fell to him to fill the position of promoter. He went to Chicago with not much more than the clothes on his back, took a bare room and put a little furniture in it to reduce the cost of living. Before the bonds were placed Mr. Greene was in straits for food. But his persuasive tongue and his thorough acquaintance with the possibilities of irrigation won. He now lives at the highest-priced hotel in New York when he is in the East looking after financial matters. He travels in a private car when he comes West. A single bond deal recently netted him $90,000.

But large profits are necessary to carry on such irrigation ideas as Mr. Greene fosters. In the suburbs of Eddy this man has a nursery, propagating houses and an outfit for creating a park. As the beginning he is laying out 240 acres with winding drives, shade and fruit trees and lawn. This he will keep under control until well established. Then

PROPAGATING HOUSES AT THE GREENE PARK.

he will divide it into residence sites and sell to those who do not know so much about irrigation as he does. When trees and grass are once well started the rest is easy. When the 240 acres are in a forward state Mr. Greene will add to it another addition similarly improved by irrigation. This collection of residence sites is called Greene Park. But the park and the 520 acres of grapes are only two he has any payments to make. The alfalfa will be paying handsomely by that time. Mr. Greene further proposes to loan the buyer money to make improvements. That is if the buyer has $500 or $1000 and wants as much more to put into improvements Mr. Greene will loan it and take a lien on the property. Some of these forty-acre tracts already have their twenty-acre patches of alfalfa. Raw land,

THE GATEWAY TO THE CANAL.

of the projects of Mr. Greene. In the valley a company, of which he is the head, has 1920 acres at one place and 3,000 acres at another. This is some of the land nobody would take from the Government. It is now reached by the laterals of the great canal. The whole 5,000 acres is being divided into forty-acre tracts. Mr. Greene clears the land of the mesquite roots, plows and ditches it. Twenty acres of the forty goes into alfalfa. Ten acres, half of the remainder, is set out to fruit, a choice assortment. When the alfalfa is well rooted and the fruit trees begin to bear Mr. Greene will sell these forty acre tracts. He knows by observation that the beginner with irrigation makes many blunders. He proposes to put each forty acres beyond the critical period and to assure the purchaser a good start before he sells. The price of the forty acres thus started will be $60 an acre, one-fourth cash, the balance in two, three and four years.

"The point is," said Mr. Russell, who looks after Mr. Greene's interests, "the purchaser get two years' cutting of the alfalfa before without anything upon it, is worth $25 to $40 an acre."

This is what water for irrigation does. The company which has dammed the river and dug the canals owns the water and sells it at $1.25 an acre for the season. An owner of forty acres of land, therefore, has $60 a year water rent, but on the payment of it he is assured perfect control of his crops if he knows how to irrigate.

Mr. Greene has spent over $150,000 in improving and preparing his lands since the 1st of December. His pay-roll ran up in one month to $12,750. One of Mr. Greene's minor enterprises is an addition of town lots, on each one of which he starts by irrigation twenty fruit trees before he sells. Scattered through the addition are eight little parks, each of which is being supplied with shrubbery.

Near where the Eddy ranch house still stands is the suburb of La Huerta, covering 1500 acres. It is divided into five-acre tracts, each one leveled, divided into alfalfa, garden and fruit, and improved to suit the taste of the owner. Each five-acre tract means the site of a fine home. Land in La Huerta is worth $100 an acre. In the gardens of La Huerta are shown some of the examples of what irrigation can do. In an orchard of last year's planting the tape line shows the growth this season on apple trees to be from 20 inches to 37 inches. On apricot trees this season's growth is 5 feet and 6 inches. A plum tree shows 23 inches growth, and a peach 38 inches. Such were the measurements when this was written. When it reaches the reader a few days hence there will be considerable more growth. There was nothing fabulous about Jack's bean stalk if it had been planted in the Pecos Valley and irrigated.

The founders of Eddy and the Pecos canal system have evidently come to stay. They are not boomers who expect to sell out and move on. The lavish manner in which Mr. Greene has spread out his profits in park and vineyards and forty-acre farms has been mentioned. All he has is here. Mr. Eddy, the original ranch-owner, who first dreamed of the possibilities which have come to pass, has built a home in interesting contrast with the old ranch headquarters. Upon an elevation overlooking the city and the valley Mr. Hagerman is constructing the finest stone mansion ever built upon a desert-land entry. The site is far above the level of the canal—so far that nobody thought of taking possession of it, even though a city was growing in the valley below. Mrs. Hagerman entered the 640 acres, a mile square, under the desert-land law. Water is taken up the height by hydraulic rams and stored in a reservoir. And there the white walls of the Hagerman mansion are rising.

Hagerman is a fine type of the self-made Western man. Greene is fond of irrigation per se, and has studied out all the details of it. Eddy's mind runs to broad acres and the number of them. Hagerman's inclination is toward construction. His chief interest is in the dam, the canals and the railroad. The three founders of the enterprise move well abreast. They all take pride that isn't measured by dollars in the work. They let nothing come in the way of success. Awhile ago some

MEASURING GROWTH BY IRRIGATION.

people up the valley held water rights which the company wanted.
"How much will it take to buy them out?" Hagerman asked.
After some figuring the reply was, "At least $250,000."
"Buy them out," was the order.
Hagerman has a bull-dog tenacity for holding on. He is reticent. An expression of sentiment from his lips is a rarity. The other day he rode out with the manager of the company, viewing certain improvements and authorizing in his matter-of-fact way expenditures here and there. Toward the end of the drive the magnate and the manager ascended an elevation. The whole scene was spread before them—the city, the farms, the railroad, the canals. The manager stopped the team, and in silence a long look was taken. At length the manager asked:
"How does it strike you Mr. Hagerman?"
"Mr. Clark, it touches me right here," responded the man of few words, and he put his hand on his heart.
It cost Mr. Hagerman $11,000 to get the water up to Mrs. Hagerman's desert-land en-

try. He is spending $50,000 on the stone mansion. That is pretty good evidence of an intention to stay.

Alfalfa! alfalfa! It is the open sesame of the Pecos Valley. You see it everywhere, and hear about it after dark when you can't see it. The landholder who hasn't a patch of alfalfa is unhappy. Alfalfa is aggressive; it chokes out all weeds; when it is once well rooted it is there to stay, with an occasional wetting from the ditch. The alfalfa growers have never yet overstocked their market. They get $12 a ton—sometimes more, sometimes a little less, but always a handsome profit. They cut it three and four times a year, and get from one to two, and sometimes two and a half tons to the acre each time. Alfalfa is clover, and its blossom furnishes the flavor for a honey that is nectar. One man in the Pecos Valley has grasped the situation. He has surrounded his house with colonies of bees which improve the shining hours upon the alfalfa fields of his neighbors. The days on the Rio Pecos—"Holy River," so named by a priest in the Cortez following who came here and found the natives keeping alive beside it the holy fire for the return of a dimly remembered Messiah—are long and cloudless. Bees do not need the aid of lightning bugs to lengthen their hours of labor. In a few years half of this Pecos Valley will be in alfalfa, and then what train loads of honey will leave it for the Eastern markets!

Before they stop digging ditches the men at the head of the enterprise say they will bring the water to 400,000 acres of land. And when that is done there will be 200,000 acres of alfalfa growing along the Pecos. What in the world will be done with it? The busy thinkers have already figured on that proposition. They say that alfalfa will not go below $8 or $10 a ton. Last year the cattlemen near the

THE EDDY RANCH.

valley drove their steers into pens, fed them alfalfa from November to February, and put them into market rolling fat, thereby competing with the corn-fed steers of Kansas. These steers were worth from $14 to $17 taken from the range. Fattened on alfalfa they sold at $35 to $50 a head. They ate two tons of alfal-

THE PECOS VALLEY AT THE DAM.

fa. There is the basis on which it is figured that alfalfa will always be worth at least $8 a ton along the Pecos, for 300,000 cattle and 100,000 sheep range within fifty miles of the valley. At $8 a ton for alfalfa the farmer can pay for labor and water rental and net $40 per acre. Such are the alluring figures presented with great confidence by those who have faith in the future of the holy river. W. B. S.

THROUGH TEXAS.

Queer Industries in the Heart of the Late Great American Desert.

A Canaigre Farm—Nature's Salt Works —Cactus Rope—How One man Kept Tab on Irrigation—A Great Show.

Special Correspondence of the Globe-Democrat.

IN THE PECOS VALLEY OF TEXAS, August 18.— The traveler in this region will occasionally come upon a group of tents, a portable engine, a little mill, a great heap of tangled roots and a curious looking product spread out on sheets to dry. This is the canaigre industry. Indians have known, perhaps for centuries, the uses of canaigre. Americans have within a year or so discovered that it can be made an article of commerce. And now canaigre root, ground and dried and put up in sacks, is shipped out of the Pecos Valley by the carload. It goes abroad. From the rapid development of the industry it appears that there must be a good margin of profit.

every pound that can be turned out. Canaigre root as it flourishes in the valley is gathered at a cost of $4 to $6 per ton. An acre of canaigre in the wild state will yield six to eight tons. The curing is simple. When the outfit exhausts one locality it can strike tents, pick up the engine and mill and move to a new field. The cured product is worth $80 a ton in Europe. The demand seems to be permanent and the margin of profit is good. One man in the Pecos Valley has gone into the business on a permanent basis. He has a canaigre farm of 640 acres—a mile square. From such experiments as have been made, this canaigre farmer believes he will obtain ten to twenty tons of roots from an acre by cultivation. Beets give a tremendous yield on this irrigated land. As much as twenty-six tons of beets to the acre was produced last year. There is reason to believe that canaigre roots will do almost as well. Heaped up the canaigre roots look not unlike a crop of beets. They grind easily and dry quickly spread out on sheets under the blazing sun. After that, all that remains to be done is the sacking. The product is ready for market. The canaigre industry is using up the wild root faster than it reproduces itself. Unless there is cultivation the industry can not but be short-lived.

THE DIABLO MOUNTAINS AT VAN HORN.

Canaigre is a close relative of the sour dock which is found in the fields of the North. Above ground the canaigre makes only a moderate show of stalk and leaves. Below ground it spreads itself and grows until it develops roots as large as a man's arm. It has been growing wild in this Pecos Valley ever since white men knew anything about the country. But it is recently that those who deal in such things have learned that it contains four times as much tannin as anything else that vegetates. Mr. Donald Allen, the Superintendent of the Pecos Valley Railroad, called the attention of exporters to this product, and now there is a profitable market for

This Western Texas is a great country for new industries. It is even proposed to utilize the cactus, which grows in great variety and luxuriance on the mountain sides. One kind, called the Spanish bayonet, is 3 feet high. It is a broad-leaf plant. Another and shorter variety is the mescal plant. From this the Mexican makes his mescal, a fiery liquid, which will nerve the drinker to rob the dead or run for Congress if he takes enough of it. The leaves of these varieties of cactus have been worked up into fiber which makes good rope. Some of the products of the cactus fiber from Western Texas have been prepared for exhibition at the World's Fair next year.

A part of the leaf is left as it grows and the other end is shown in the condition of fiber. The contrast is striking. The trunk of the Spanish bayonet contains good paper stock. These varieties of cactus grow wild, and the enterprising people of the transpecos country are beginning to wonder if cultivation will not add to their value. A cactus farm would be a novelty, but it is not an impossibility. The cactus fiber in the manufactured state looks very strong and durable. The only question is about the cost of getting the fiber out of the thick pulpy looking leaves. Machinery, it is claimed, can be devised to do the work. Industrial uses for the cactus are novelties. When drouth comes and grass dies the lives of herds are often prolonged in Southwest Texas by the use of cactus for forage. A starving longhorn cow, with an expression of desperate determination, will gingerly mouth and at length masticate a piece of cactus, thorns and all. But the humane cowman cuts the cactus and gives it just enough roasting with a quick fire to burn the thorns before feeding. There is better forage than cactus, but the latter will, on pinch, keep life in the hide. The Panhandle cowman says a cactus patch is considered a very desirable thing on a Southwest Texas ranch.

Texas cattle are licking Texas salt by the car load. Five or six years ago the people of Colorado City, away out on the rugged bluffs of the Colorado River, felt that they had reached a degree of advancement which justified municipal airs. They thought they ought to have a City Council. When they got that, they discovered that their water supply wasn't what it ought to be. There came in a class of high-toned settlers who weren't satisfied with whisky and water, but wanted all water, and good water, too. The City Council in due deliberation moved in the matter. A considerable fund was raised, and a deep hole was bored. The drill went down 1200 feet. It didn't find good drinking water, but it struck petroleum, 80 feet of rock salt and other things. The boring stopped for awhile. Colorado City offered its hole for sale, but found no takers. After awhile somebody thought of making use of the salt. The hole was bored deeper. It struck fresh water which arose to within 200 or 300 feet of the surface and dissolved the rock salt. A pump was put down. A wind-

THE CANAIGRE INDUSTRY.

mill was hoisted above the pump. The wind raised the salt water which was run into a reservoir. This West Texas sun which shines about 340 days in the year did the rest. Colorado City had salt. Other wells have been bored. Windmills have been hoisted in rows until Don Quixote might think he saw, by the moonlight, a whole army defying him. The process commends itself to an economical, not to say a

MOVING UP THE PECOS VALLEY.

lazy man. The water dissolves the rock salt. The wind raises the water. The sun evaporates the water and leaves the salt on the ground. Could anything be easier? Manual labor is necessary to scrape up the salt and barrel it, and that is all. A 30-foot windmill raises from 5,000 to 8,000 gallons of salt water in an hour. Of the salt thus manufactured by nature's forces Colorado City ships out several hundred car loads a month. A chemical analysis shows this salt to be 98 per cent pure. In a country where there was less sunshine and wind salt-making could not be carried on so successfully.

The talk of the promoter is interesting, but not always satisfying as to detail. The average farmer is inclined to tell of his big crops and not of the small ones, unless he is in the investment and wear and tear of tools. One might search long, especially in this free and easy Western country, without finding another such analysis of work with irrigation.

NATURE'S SALT WORKS AT COLORADO CITY.

third party. A farm on which books are kept with the same thoroughness that the successful merchant exercises is a great rarity. There is one such farm near Pecos City. It is only forty acres, and of this only thirty-three have been cultivated. The owner has put down the cents and pounds. As might be supposed,

AN ARTESIAN SPOUTER AT PECOS CITY.

he is not a practical farmer. He has other business. His commercial habits prompted him to keep a strict account. All of the farm work was done by hired men. The balance sheet takes into consideration interest on the

Here is the showing for a single season on the forty acres, with thirty-three in crops:

To 8 per cent interest on $2,394.65, cost of lands, water rights, orchard, canals, borders, tools, houses, fencing, etc.	$191 57
Twenty-five per cent wear on $297.50 worth of implements	71 87
Harvesting and baling alfalfa	178 00
Harvesting oats	80 00
Seeding and harvesting garden	350 00
Seeding five acres in grain	30 00
Irrigating farm one year	30 20
Seeding and harvesting oats, millet and sorghum	80 00
Total outlay	$961 64
Cabbage, 1033 pounds at 6c	61 98
Turnips, 549 pounds at 4c	21 96
Beets, 593 pounds at 3c	17 79
Sweet potatoes, 1856 pounds at 4c	54 24
Squashes, 285 pounds at 4c	11 40
Sorghum hay, 12¼ tons at $15	183 75
Muskmelons, 305 at 5c	15 25
Prairie hay, 12 tons at $15	225 00
Millet hay, 6125 pounds at $15 per ton	45 93
Watermelons, 421 at 15c	63 15
Oats in sheaf, 34,330 pounds at $15 per ton	257 47
Alfalfa, 178,672 pounds at $15 per ton	1,340 04
Onions, 7837 pounds at 4c	313 48
Irish potatoes, 541 pounds at 4c	21 64
Peanuts, 440 pounds at 7½c	33 00
	$2,666 08
Deduct total outlay	961 64
Cash balance to profit	$1,704 44

This, it can readily be figured, is a return of about 75 per cent on the investment. It is a net profit of $51.65 cash per acre. The fun which this amateur farmer enjoyed is not taken into account. He says that if he had lived on the place he could have added at least

$500 from poultry, pigs and the usual small items. Being a man of details he probably could have done it.

East of the Pecos, between that river and the Colorado, lies the country of deceptions. It is the great Staked Plain which stretches away to the Panhandle. The air is dry and clear. A mountain forty miles away seems to be not one-fourth that distance. A good pair of eyes will see twice as far and about ten times as much in this region as under ordinary conditions. If the vision doesn't embrace a good many unrealities as well as realities it will be an unusual day for the Staked Plain. The atmosphere plays freaks as well as makes revelations. When the sun is just right it is possible to see a belt of timber where none exists. A ranch may be lifted out of a valley and set on a hill. A sheep herder grows into gigantic proportions and his lambs become elephantine. A railroad train in the distance looms up a hundred feet high, and appears to be about five miles long. These are some of the common deceptions the rarified atmosphere of the Staked Plain plays upon the tenderfoot. Three or four miles to the eastward of Midland, if it be about noon of a sunny day, the stranger will see a fine little city in the midst of a glistening lake. The silvery water moves in ripples as if before a gentle breeze. About 300 windmills are apparently in motion above the city, and it does not seem that the space they stand upon can exceed a mile square. Around the city and the lake is a fringe of dark green timber. Beyond the timber is a boundless expanse of green grass. On the prairie cattle may be seen grazing. The traveler, reflecting upon the lake and the excess of windmills, may wonder if the Midlanders are web-footed that they have so many windmills and raise water until their houses are swamped. But as the train comes nearer what strangeness! The

A PECOS VALLEY HOME.

cows in the foreground grow to mastodons. The jack rabbit is as large as a jack without the rabbit. The sheep seem to be woolly horses. The buildings shoot up into the heavens like Chicago's sky-scrapers. The windmills become so many Eiffel towers standing on nothing. The people walking across the street tread on air. There is no law of gravity. The lake has suddenly disappeared. The traveler steps from the car upon a real platform and out upon the dusty, sandy thoroughfare of an every-day Texas town. It was the mirage. W. B. S.

THROUGH TEXAS.

A Visit to the Only Survivor of the Bold Buccaneers.

The Veteran Cronea's Recollections of Service with the Pirates.

Lafitte and His Favorite Lieutenant—The Freebooter's Camp on Snake Island.

The Mutiny on the Privateer—A Graphic Version of San Jacinto—Four Generations on One Porch—Bolivar Peninsula Phenomena—The High Islands—The Oil Ponds.

Special Correspondence of the Globe-Democrat.

ROLL OVER, BOLIVAR PENINSULA, TEX., August 25.—At the age of 87, Charles Cronea remembers the name of the street and the number of the house in which he was born in a town of the South of France. He is the last living link with the days of Lafitte and the bold buccaneers of the Gulf. Seventy-one years ago he was a cabin boy on a pirate ship. He sailed these waters with Campbell, who had been Lafitte's lieutenant. He saw many a chase at sea. He was there when the "Long Tom," mounted on a pivot, sent the huge 18-pound ball across the bow of the doomed merchantman. He saw the torch applied to the prize, and the choicest part of the cargo brought aboard the privateer. After a mutiny he waited for the cutlass to fall across his neck, and then lived to see ninety-two children, grandchildren and great-grandchildren. The scenes of those days come back to the old man with wonderful freshness. He talks freely, stopping now and then to explain that it was "an ugly scrape," and that when he got out of it he had "had enough of that kind of thing to last him all his life."

A strip of land runs down the Texas coast from near the Louisiana line. That is Bolivar Peninsula. It terminates in Bolivar Point. Five miles across a channel from "the point" Galveston Island begins and the City of Galveston has its site. About midway of its length Bolivar Peninsula narrows until upon the map it is only a black line. That is Roll Over. Upon Roll Over is the home of Charles Cronea. When the Gulf is angry its spray is dashed against the old man's front door. From his back door stretches the great Galveston Bay. The veteran is as near to the salt water as he can get without being afloat.

To Roll Over was a journey not soon to be forgotten. It began an hour before daylight. When the sun came up out of the bosom of the Gulf the White Wings, best of the Galveston yacht fleet, was speeding with well-filled sails straight for the tall white and black ringed light-house on Bolivar point. Bolivar once had a boom. "The point" was staked off and town lots were put upon the market. With that the boom ended. There are not enough people living at the point now to occupy the houses which the Government built when it was constructing jetties on the mattress plan. A small boat yard, where the craft which ply the bay can be hauled out and

MR. CRONEA AT 87.

repaired, is the point's only industry. Broadway and the town lots are unsettled save by mosquitoes, remarkable for numbers, size and aggressiveness.

When Mr. Pettit, of Galveston, a friend of the old veteran, learned of the intended visit, he said: "I'd advise you to wait a week. The mosquitoes are awful bad on Bolivar just now. There has been rain and the wind has blown from the north. That always means mosquitoes."

Mr. Pettit's warning could not be heeded. It was well remembered. The early morning sail was magnificent. The ride across the flat from the point to the light house was misery. Mr. Crockett, the light-house keeper, came out with a serious face.

"Last night," said he, "Was the worst of the season. We had to keep smudge fires going all night long to save the horses. If you take the beach I expect you can get along. But I wouldn't advise you to try the ridge road."

The light-house keeper cut a mosquito-bar in two, and, like a good Samaritan, saw that heads and faces were well covered. He brought out gloves and stockings to be drawn over the hands. He furnished a bottle of coal oil. Then the battle with the mosquitoes of Bolivar began. It lasted until the beach was reached. Before, behind and on both sides of the wagon went the mosquitoes. They made no noise. These Bolivar mosquitoes are not singers. They are too full of business to waste time on music. There was one honorable way out of the contest. The son of the lighthouse man, who accompanied us as guide,

WHITE WINGS.

philosopher and friend, knew that way. By the shortest cut he made for the beach and drove down to the water's edge, where the light surf coming in washed the wheels. And thus he followed the water line hour after hour. The mosquitoes were outwitted. Before the damp salt breeze they fell back. It was a great relief, the full measure of which was appreciated every time a little excursion was made inland. Ten thousand cattle were strung along the surf line, hugging it closely to escape the mosquitoes. They, too, had discovered the only possible relief.

The light-house man's boy is an authority on mosquitoes. He pointed out a section of the peninsula where he confidently asserted mosquitoes live the year round. Bolivar is famous for its climate. Lying between the waters of gulf and bay, it is a region of almost perpetual vegetation. Frost is of the rarest occurrence. Oranges and pomegranates thrive, and the "early vegetables" antedate Florida's crop. There may be beaches equal to that along Bolivar peninsula. There can be none better. As the tide goes out it leaves a stretch of white sand, pounded by the surf as hard as asphalt. The wheels make a mark, but cut no impression. So slight is the dip toward the sea that the beach seems a dead level. And this roadway of nature can be followed straight as the crow flies hour after hour.

The origin of the name of Roll Over is interesting. Some people will tell you that by reason of the narrowness of the peninsula at this point the high waves of the Gulf have been known to roll over the neck and into the bay. But the old inhabitants have an entirely different explanation. They say that the smugglers and pirates used to bring their plunder from the Gulf to this place. The smugglers could quickly roll over the casks of brandy and the bales of goods from the Gulf side to the bay, and thus reach inland waters and their market without detection. Old Mr. Cronea, with a laugh, said he reckoned the theory of the smuggling use of Roll Over was about right. "That is the way I think it got the name," he said.

The veteran was born in 1805, on the 14th of January. He was only a boy when he found himself in the pirate service, but his recollections are clear. Some of the places he mentions have faded almost out of memory, or have new names. To some of his words the old man gives a pronunciation which has a distinctly piratical flavor. Cutlasses he always calls "cut-lash-es." The bayonet is always "the bagnet." And occasionally he "swears like a pirate," in the gentlest of voices.

Hanging on the wall of the Roll Over home is a picture of the old man taken at 70. It shows that he comes well by his remarkable preservation. He shakes his head half mournfully and says "you should have seen my legs and arms a few years ago. My arms were so big and as hard as iron. Now feel them" The eyes are hazel. They were as black as the sloe-like windows of the soul through which the great grandson looks wonderingly to-day. The veteran's hair is long, wavy, thin and silvery. It was thick, bushy and jet black. But the mind has outlived the body. The old man speaks quickly and decidedly. He is at no loss for words or ideas. He talked for two hours without any apparent feeling of fatigue and then he said: "There, that's all I can tell you." But a question started a fresh train of reminiscences. The stock was almost inexhaustible.

Before he was 12 years old Charles Cronea was on a French frigate. He served awhile on the coast of Africa, and then left without waiting for the formalities. He reached New York and shipped as cabin boy on a vessel going to Charleston. His captain took on a load of cotton. To his consternation the boy learned that the destination was Havre de Grace. This meant capture and the penalty for the French leave he had taken of the frigate.

came to us. His ship was there at anchor. He talked to us awhile and we went on board his ship and served with him. I was too young to be one of the crew. He made me a cabin boy."

That was young Cronea's introduction to the buccaneers. During his service he saw many ships taken, plundered and burned. "Capt. Campbell," said Mr. Cronea, "was a good man. He would not kill any of the crews. He always made them prisoners, took

BOLIVAR POINT.

"I left the ship," continued the old man, "and went on board one going to Liverpool. That was what Capt. Lambert said, but when we got outside of Charleston harbor a man who called himself Jones came aboard and said he wanted some of us to go with him. Our captain seemed perfectly willing. I suppose it was well understood between him and our captain. Fifteen of us agreed to go with Jones. There was one Catalonian in the party. The rest of us were French. We went with Jones and he sailed away for the Gulf of Mexico. When he arrived off Corpus Christi he landed us on an island and left some food with us. After awhile Capt. Campbell them to some point near the coast and put them in small boats so that they could get ashore. Most of the vessels we captured were in the trade between Tampico and the Island of Cuba."

"Didn't you have some fighting to make the captures?"

"Oh, no. They always gave up. It wasn't any use to resist."

"You were prepared to fight if it was necessary?"

"Yes, we had pistols, the old-fashioned one-barreled kind, with flints. We also had cutlash-es. They were big things, as keen as a razor. They weighed about five pounds

When one of those knives came down it was good-bye Coly."

"What sort of a crew did you have, pretty rough?"

"We had the same discipline as on board a man-of-war. We couldn't have done what we did if it hadn't been so. Any man who misbehaved was punished."

"Did you sail under the black flag."

"Oh, no! We hoisted the flag of Carthagenia."

Both Lafitte and Campbell were particular to observe the forms of legitimate warfare. They hoisted on their vessels the flag of a struggling republic, and the letters of marque under which they plundered right and left, and the fore mast had the square sails of the brig. This gave speed and it also permitted of the peculiar armament. The big gun was mounted in front of the mast and it could be wheeled to point in almost any direction except in the rear.

The old man's eyes twinkled as he told of some of the feats of the clipper from Baltimore. "Campbell's ship," said he, "could sail fourteen miles an hour on a close haul. There wasn't anything that could get away from her. Once we took after the mail boat between Tampico and New Orleans. We overtook her in about two hours and spoke her. As soon as Capt. Campbell learned that she was an American vessel he let her go."

A MOSQUITO CHASE.

were more or less regular. Lafitte was a blacksmith to begin with in New Orleans. He adopted smuggling, which was very popular on the Louisiana coast, and when afterwards he set up his establishment on Galveston Island, he had a fleet and a thousand followers.

John Quincy Adams in his diary tells of a visit he made to Baltimore. Upon investigation he discovered that the merchants of that city were engaged quite generally in fitting out vessels to engage in privateering on the Gulf of Mexico. He says it inspired a peculiar feeling to find that his entertainers were in this strange business. Mr. Cronea says that the vessel on which he served under Capt. Campbell was from Baltimore. The craft was known as an hermaphrodite brig. She had two masts. The rear mast was sloop-rigged

Campbell, like his chief, Lafitte, would never interfere with an American ship. That was the unwritten law of the pirates of the gulf. Lafitte always considered himself an American. In the State Capitol at Baton Rouge hangs a large oil painting commemorative of the battle of New Orleans. In the very thickest of the fight, directing the work of a battery, is a gigantic figure which is pointed out to the visitor as that of Lafitte, the pirate. It is history that Lafitte fought most bravely under Gen. Jackson in that decisive battle of the War of 1812, and that a pardon was issued to him for it. Before that a price had been set upon Lafitte's head, and his brother had been thrown into prison by the American Governor of Louisiana. The commander of the British forces approaching the mouth of the Mississippi sent to the chief of the smugglers, then having his headquarters at Barataria, an offer of $30,000 to join him. He added this message:

"I call upon you, with your brave followers, to enter the service of Great Britain, in which you shall have the rank of captain. Lands will be given you all, in proportion to your respective ranks, on peace taking place, and I invite you upon these terms. Your ships to be placed under the commanding officer of this station, but I guarantee their full value at all events."

Lafitte, keeping up the form of negotiations, wrote a member of the Louisiana Legislature: "Though proscribed by my adopted country I will never let slip any occasion of serving her. Of this you will see convincing proof."

To the Governor who had put a price on his head the pirate sent this message:

"I am a stray sheep, wishing to return to the sheep fold. If you were thoroughly acquainted with the nature of my offenses, I should appear to you much less guilty and still worthy to discharge the duties of a good citizen. I have never sailed under any flag but the Republic of Carthagena, and my vessels are perfectly regular in that respect. If I could have orought in my prizes into the ports of this State I should not have employed the illicit means that have caused me to be proscribed. I decline saying more on the subject until I have the honor of your Excellency's answer. Should you not answer favorably to my ardent desires I declare that I will instantly leave the country to avoid the imputation of having co-operated toward an invasion which can not fail to take place, and rest secure in the acquittal of my conscience."

That is good language for a pirate. A committee of safety ignored the proceedings of the Governor against Lafitte, and assured him immunity for his past. Gen. Jackson gave the Baratarian leader a post of great danger. To the work which the pirate band did with their guns history attributes much of the credit for that victory on the 8th of January. The promise of immunity was kept. Lafitte's past and that of his followers was condoned. But not long afterwards the United States Government sent a message to the pirate that he must move from Barataria or behave. On that warning Lafitte with his followers broke up the old headquarters, sailed down the Texas coast, and settled on the island which is now the site of Galveston. There the leader ruled a colony of buccaneers and there Campbell joined him.

Lafitte lived in a red house which he built near what is now the foot of Fifteenth street, in Galveston. He threw up breastworks around the house and mounted some cannon. The colony grew until a thousand men made their homes on the island and acknowledged allegiance to no living person save Lafitte. The ships of these buccaneers preyed on the Spanish commerce of the whole Gulf of Mexico. Mr. Adams need have had no such squeamishness over the fact that his Baltimore hosts were the silent partners of Lafitte. The goods which the buccaneers captured and smuggled into the United States were handled by many Boston merchants who were not

THE YOUNG IDEA IN BOLIVAR.

above being "fences" for pirates. Lafitte had his agents in New Orleans; they went on 'Change daily, and orders were given them openly for the goods which they had to dispose of. Boston, Baltimore and other commercial centers were ready "partakers."

When the freebooters' camp on Galveston Island was at the height of its glory Lafitte was a man of about 40. He was over 6 feet in height, strongly built, handsome of features, hazel eyes and black hair. In manner he was very polite. It was a motley gathering of outlaws, but Lafitte ruled them in the same free and easy way that Robin Hood did his merry men. There was always a square divide of the prize money, and contentment reigned on the island. Several miles down the island, below the suburbs of Galveston, is a grove of live oaks visible a long way out on the water. This is known as Lafitte's Grove. Tradition has it that the pirates often assembled under the shade to divide their booty.

The freebooters were not without a form of government on the island. They called themselves subjects of the republic under the flag of which they sailed. They elected one freebooter "Judge of the Admiralty," another "Administrator of the Revenue," a third "Secretary of the Public Treasury," a fourth "Marine Commandant," and so on. But Lafitte was king pirate, and his word was law. The man who held the high-sounding office of "Judge of the Admiralty," had occasion, years afterward to make a statement about this colony. It was to the effect that "the sole view and object of the persons comprising the colony was to capture Spanish vessels and property, without any idea of aiding the revolution in Mexico or that of any other of the revolted Spanish colonies." The freebooters called their town Campeachy. The island went by the name of Snake Island because of the number of serpents.

When the light-house rig stopped in front of the Cronea homestead a brilliantly colored rattlesnake lay coiled up in the sand beside the wheel.

To show how perfect was Lafitte's power over his followers the story of Capt. Brown is told. Brown came to the island and sought permission to cruise under Lafitte's auspices. Lafitte suspected Brown, and when he gave him his orders told him that if he molested the commerce of the United States he would hang him. With many promises Brown set sail. Several days afterward Brown and his crew, half starved, appeared at Bolivar Point and signaled for help. They were conveyed to the freebooters' camp and Lafitte examined the men. He learned from them that Brown had robbed an American vessel near Sabine Pass. A revenue schooner had pursued. Brown had beached his boat, and had walked down the peninsula. Without any delay Lafitte had Brown hung in chains. He left the body suspended for the buzzards to feed upon. The revenue schooner sailed to the freebooters' camp. The commander went ashore and demanded the fugitives. Lafitte at once surrendered the crew, and pointing toward the swinging figure in iron said: "You will find the captain over there."

Occasionally Lafitte's vessel captured slavers. Some who paid allegiance to the pirate king were in the slave trade. Upon the arrival of a cargo of human chattels at Snake Island a curious scene was witnessed. Louisiana planters were notified and came to the market. The negroes were sold by weight. The ruling rate in the freebooters' camp was $1 a pound. The planters drove the negroes they purchased to the frontier of the United States. There they delivered them into the hands of a customs officer, becoming informers. Under the law the informer was entitled to half of the amount realized on the seized property. The negroes were sold at auction by the United States Marshal. They were bid in by the original purchasers and informers, who thus obtained a clear legal title and the right to take their property where they pleased as the reward for their observance of the technicalities. One Louisiana slave dealer boasted of making $65,000 in a short time by thus smuggling slaves from Lafitte's camp into the United States.

LAFITTE.

The time came when the United States determined that the freebooters' camp must go. An American vessel was plundered and scuttled in Matagorda Bay. In spite of the pirate king's orders his followers did not always stop to inquire as to the nationality of a victim. Representatives of foreign powers complained at Washington about the ravages of Lafitte's fleet. A United States brig was sent to break up the camp. Lafitte went out to meet the commanding officer and escorted him over the bar. He entertained him handsomely at "the red house." The naval officer communicated his orders. Lafitte said he would obey. In the presence of the representative of the United States there was a grand distribution of prize money. The organization was disbanded. The torch was applied to the buildings and the fire burned until the camp was in ruins. Then the fleet of pirate ships was brought together. Lafitte's favorite ship—The Bride—was put in readiness. Those freebooters who wished went with Lafitte. The others scattered. The king pirate in his flagship, with the fleet following, sailed away. He never returned to Texas. He settled on the coast of Yucatan, where he was given a concession of land for his "services on behalf of Mexican independence," and "where he lived in peace till he died." In his old age he reformed. So did many of his followers. Years afterward, when Galveston was settled by Americans who came there to lead honest lives, there was a character about the wharves who went by the name of Ben Dolliver. Ben had a brother named Jim.

MR. CRONEA AT 70.

It was the common understanding of the Galveston people that Ben and Jim Dolliver were sons of a New England minister, and that they had been pirates under Lafitte. Ben was a little bit of a dried-up fellow with a cock eye. On a certain occasion there sailed into Galveston harbor a war vessel from some Central American nation. The captain's name was Cox. He wore a splendid uniform, had an elegant sword and looked like a grandee. Commander Cox was received with distinction. One day he was on Tremont street conversing with some of the first citizens of Galveston. Ben Dolliver came rolling by. He lurched up in front of the big commander in gold lace and sword, and after close scrutiny called out in his squeaky voice:

"I know you. You're a d——d pirate."

With a terrible oath the commander drew his sword and ran at Ben. The little fellow jumped out in the middle of the street, shoved his hand into one of his wide-topped boots he wore and pulled a murderous looking knife. It was the big commander's turn to run, and he made good time until a saloon door sheltered him. Ben had recognized an old comrade of the freebooting days.

One of old man Cronea's most thrilling stories is of the mutiny which occurred on Campbell's privateer. Next in command to Capt. Campbell was Lieut. Duvall. This trouble occurred shortly before the breaking up of the crew.

"Duvall's idea," said Mr. Cronea, "was to put to death the captain and the old crew, and take possession of the vessel with the fifteen who joined the force when I did. I don't know what he meant to do after that. I knew there was going to be a mutiny, but I didn't know it was going to take place that night. The men that Duvall got to go into the mutiny were French, except one; he was the Catalonian. The old crew were all Americans. Duvall hauled up a cask of brandy and gave it to the men. If it hadn't been for that he might have succeeded, but the brandy spoiled it all. The men Duvall had were on watch when the attack was made. The others and the captain were below. Duvall and his men could have called up the captain and killed him or made him a prisoner. Then they could have got the arms which the captain always kept in the cabin and could have killed the others as fast as they came on deck. They made the attack just about night. I was looking out of the cabin and saw it all. Campbell went on deck and the mutineers surrounded him. But they were drunk and didn't have any plan. Some wanted to kill the captain right there. Others were for letting him go or making him a prisoner. While they were quarreling about what they would do with him he put out his arms, just so, brushed them to both sides of him, made one jump and landed in the cabin By that time the Americans, who were not in the plot, came up on deck. The captain handed out the arms and the mutineers didn't last any time. The whole fourteen of them were killed. The Catalonian was the only one who made a good fight. He had a knife in each hand. He jumped in between two of the

MOTIVE POWER ON BOLIVAR PENINSULA.

Americans and struck at both of them at the same time, killing them. Those were the only Americans who were killed. The Catalonian didn't get a chance to do any more. His head was taken off with a cutlash. Duvall was the only one of the mutineers who wasn't killed. They had a trial on board and condemned him to be shot, but Campbell interfered and saved his life. When the ship was off Galveston Island the captain put Duvall into a boat and sent two men with instructions to land him and come back. There was a ship at Galveston and we couldn't tell what she was. The captain was afraid to go in. While the two men were gone with Duvall we saw a large yawl coming out toward us. The captain got the crew together and asked them what they thought had better be done. They agreed that it was dangerous to take any chances, for we were very short-handed. Half of the crew had been killed in the mutiny. So the captain ordered the ship under way and we left without waiting for the two men who had gone with the small boat to land Duvall. We never heard of them again."

was in that desperate business," Mr. Cronea said. "The morning after the mutiny the Americans wanted to kill me. They said I was one of the party of Frenchmen and must have known of the plotting. They got around me and raised the cutlashes over me and were going to cut my head off, when Capt. Campbell interfered. He told them I was in the cabin and didn't know anything about it. Then they let me off."

Campbell was Lafitte's right-hand man. He came from Maryland. His parents lived on Chesapeake Bay, near Baltimore, and he was brought up as a sailmaker. In 1812 the young

FOUR GENERATIONS ON ONE PORCH.

"I don't think Campbell made a great deal out of the business," said Mr. Cronea, in reply to a question. "I remember once that he loaded up a vessel with goods that had been taken, put some of the men aboard and started it off somewhere. They didn't tell me where it was to go. But no word ever came back from it that I heard. After he quit he lived very quietly."

Mr. Cronea describes Campbell as a man of 6 feet, well built, with dark mustache and a Celtic face. "He was a very brave man, and he didn't like to see life taken, although he

sailmaker joined the United States navy. In the battle of Lake Erie Campbell was on the Lawrence with Perry. When the Commodore was forced to leave the Lawrence and take his flag to the Niagara, Campbell was one of the crew that rowed the boat in which Perry stood holding the flag half a mile under heavy fire. After the war Campbell went back to Baltimore, but only to start out on a roving expedition which took him to New Orleans. There, with his knowledge of sea life, he soon got into the smuggling business. There was nothing strange about that. Half of the merchants in New Orleans were taking goods from smugglers regularly. When Gov. Claiborne, of Louisiana, attempted to create public sentiment against this kind of vocation, he had a queer experience. Writing of it on one occasion to the Attorney General of the United States, the Governor said: "In conversation with ladies I have denounced smuggling as dishonest, and the reply was: 'That is impossible, for my grandfather, or my father, or my husband was under the Spanish Government a smuggler, and I am sure he was an honest man.'"

After Mexican independence was acknowledged, Campbell determined to give up privateering, Mr. Cronea says. There was, in admit he had ever seen me before. He wouldn't talk about what he had done. He wouldn't admit he had been on a privateer."

His service as cabin boy on the pirate ship was not the only exciting chapter in the old man's history. Charles Cronea was in the war of Texan independence from beginning to end. He is the only survivor of the bold buccaneers of the Gulf, and he is one of the few still living who "remembered Fannin's men and the Alamo" at San Jacinto. Santa Anna had wiped out the defenders of the Alamo at San Antonio to a man. He was crowding Sam Houston and the remnant of the Texan army eastward, determined not to

THE VETERAN AT HOME.

fact, nothing else for him to do. The letters of marque which gave his commerce destroying a show of legitimacy were revoked. He sailed to a point near the coast of Louisiana where there was a famous hackberry tree. There he burned the ship and disbanded the crew.

"A good ship like that couldn't be bought for $10,000," said Mr. Cronea. "It was h— to burn her. What else could he do? He couldn't go anywhere else. Peace had been declared."

"On the ship," continued Mr. Cronea, "the captain always went by the name of Carroll—Charles Carroll. He never used the name of Campbell. But after he burned the ship and settled on shore he took his right name. From the day we separated at the hackberry tree I have never seen any of the crew. Capt. Campbell I met once, years afterward. Campbell moved from place to place. I never saw him until he settled at Morse's Bluff. I heard he was living there, and went over to see him. He treated me mighty nicely, but he wouldn't stop until he had driven them across the Sabine, entirely off Texas soil, and had occupied Galveston.

"There were only 800 of us left," Mr. Cronea said. "I was in Capt. David Garner's company. After the fall of the Alamo we retreated. Santa Anna was moving eastward. We must have fallen back more than 200 miles. The Mexicans had over 2000 men. They were two to one of us, and they had cannon. I don't believe Houston would have fought, only some of the boys got tired of retreating and went to him. They said if there wasn't going to be any fightin' they would quit and go home.

"'Boys,' said Houston, 'if fightin' is what you want, you shall have plenty of it. Get your dinners.'

"That was the way the battle of San Jacinto came about. We had two companies that had muskets and bagnets. The balance of us had old Kentucky flint rifles. It took about ten minutes to load 'em. But we made every shot count. We waited till 2:30 o'clock.

The d—d Mexicans always sleep after dinner, you know. And by —— we were on them before they knew it. They never got a chance to fire their cannon but once. We dropped when we saw the smoke of their guns and then jumped up and went on. They were on one hill and we were on another. From the time we broke camp we never stopped till we were right among them. I bet you we made a lot of them drop the first time we fired. When we got into close quarters every man drew his bowie-knife. Just before we started Houston gave us the word. 'Remember Fannin's men and the Alamo,' he said. Then when he saw the slaughter he rode in among us and cried out, 'Have mercy, men! For God's sake have mercy!' But he couldn't stop us. Nothing could stop us. The Mexicans threw away their guns and stopped fighting. One would drop on his knees and hold up his hands and say, 'Me no Alamo! Me no Alamo!' Off went his d—d head! They thought we were killing them because they had killed our men at the Alamo and they wanted to say they were not there."

"Were the Mexicans well armed?"

fighting done in the War of Texas Independence was almost without parallel in losses. At the battle of the Mission, south of San Antonio, the Mexicans had forty killed and sixty wounded, while the Texas loss was one killed and one wounded. A few days later, in the Battle of the Grass, the Mexican loss was fifty and the Texan loss was one. A little later, at the Alamo, of 170 Texans not one escaped Mexican vengeance. And then came San Jacinto, wiping out an army. Santa Anna, by all the rules of Texan warfare, should have perished at San Jacinto, Mr. Cronea thinks.

"One of the men in my company, Solomon Cole, captured Santa Anna," said the old veteran. "He found him hiding in the grass, took him back to San Jacinto and delivered him to Houston. If it hadn't been that Santa Anna was a Mason his hide wouldn't have held shucks. He ought to have been shot. But Santa Anna and Sam Houston were both high Masons, and Houston and the other Masons got him off in disguise. Seven of our men followed him as far as Calcasieu, in Louisiana. If they had overtaken him he wouldn't have got back to Mexico."

ROLL OVER.

"Their guns were 'scopets,' big-mouthed things, of no account. But they had bagnets and swords, and they ought to have cut us down when we got close, but they didn't. By ——," the old man exclaimed, "they just broke like turkeys, and we cut 'em down right and left with our knives. We were right among them, and every one of us was killing."

"How many Mexicans were killed, Mr. Cronea?"

"Between 1600 and 1700. We took only 300 prisoners, and there was nothing left of Santa Anna's army."

"How many Texans were killed?"

"We lost just twelve men. There is a monument to them on the San Jacinto battle-field a few miles above Houston."

The skeptical may think the old man draws the long bow a little on his figures of losses. History, well authenticated, shows that the

"We had two scouts," the old man continued, "who kept right along close to the Mexicans all of the time during that retreat, and we always knew just where Santa Anna's army was and what it was doing. They were mighty brave men. One of 'em was Bob Dunham. I'll tell you what Bob done. Right this side of Buffalo Bayou he was all alone when he came on fifteen Mexican soldiers. He made a motion with his gun and looked back as if he was giving some order. By——the whole fifteen threw down their muskets with the bagnets sticking in the ground and surrendered. He formed 'em in line and marched 'em into camp. Bob was one of the old cowboys. The devil couldn't scare him."

During the battle of San Jacinto one body of fugitives took to the river. They mired in the muddy bottom. The Texans, coming to the bank in pursuit, stood there picking off the Mexicans in the mud and water. It was butchery. The commander of the Texans gave the order again and again to stop shooting, but the men kept on. The thirst for blood could not be satisfied, it seemed. That cry, "Remember the Alamo!" kept ringing out. At last the commander of the Texans seized a gun from one of his men and leveled it. He swore he would shoot the next man who fired upon the pleading prisoners, and then the slaughter ceased.

The battle of San Jacinto didn't last an hour, Mr. Cronea says. As one of the incidents he mentions that thirty-two Mexicans were killed at the breech of a cannon they attempted to defend. So rapid was the advance the cannon was fired only once. San Jacinto established Texan independence. Mexico did not formally acknowledge this condition, but after the loss of Santa Anna's army she let this great State go as if by default, and the United States annexed it.

"We could never have succeeded in the end," said Mr. Cronea, "if the United States had not come forward and taken up our fight. There were only 800 of us under Houston. We wiped out Santa Anna's army, it is true, but do you suppose a country as large as Mexico would have allowed 800 men to take away such a piece of territory as Texas? It isn't reasonable. We would have been crushed sooner or later if Texas had not been taken into the United States."

There was trouble from the earliest times between the Americans who had settled in Texas and the Mexican local authorities. But the open hostilities which led to the series of battles ending with San Jacinto, Mr. Cronea says, started in 1832 with the release of three Americans. These Americans were Monroe Edwards, Patrick Jack and Travers. They had been locked up by the Mexicans at the old fort of Anahuac. A company of Americans, of whom Mr. Cronea was one, was formed to release the three men and did it. After that came the battles. One of the last incidents of the Texan war took place at the home of those three men. Following San Jacinto a party stopped for the night with Monroe Edward's family. There was a young lady in the family. Her name was Susannah. Now, Susannah had a well-trained parrot. This bird had the freedom of the house during the day, but at night was retired to a cage by his young mistress. On the evening of the arrival of the visitors there was a good deal of confusion. Everybody was talking of the great battle. Miss Susannah forgot her charge, and the parrot remained out long after the usual retiring hour. At length his green-feathered Majesty's patience became exhausted. He suddenly called out "S'sannah." One of the guests sprang to his feet and looked in the direction of the sound. Then, seeing the parrot, he sat down and tried to laugh it off. The action created some curiosity at the time. But it was not till long afterward that the Edwards family learned that they had entertained Santa Anna in his disguise and on his way out of Texas under friendly escort of the Masons, in whose care Houston had placed the prisoner. Santa Anna had mistaken the parrot's call for his own name.

"Mr. Cronea, how do you account for your long life and good health?" the old man was asked as he concluded his story of the battle.

"Oh, I don't know," he replied with a hearty laugh.

"I'll tell you, sir," said a jolly, plump woman with a rich olive complexion, not a wrinkle in it, and with snapping black eyes. She came forward from the domestic regions, where she had overheard the question. "I'll tell you," she said. "It's living in the country on good healthy food—corn bread, beef and potatoes. That has given father long life and good health."

"I expect that's it," the old man added with a nod. "That is what I raised my family on. Many of my children never saw wheat flour until after they were grown."

"I think the rich food city people eat—the preserves and such things—has a good deal to do with the sickness and short lives," said the jolly lady. "I am 56 years old. Yes, sir; I own up to it. I was born the next year after the war of Texan independence. That makes me 56, and I can tell you I was 26 years old before I ever had a headache. Perhaps I wouldn't be so free to tell my age if I hadn't so many grandchildren.

The lady laughed until she shook, while the old gentleman, taking up the theme, said: "I was married to her mother after I quit the Texas army. I have now ninety living children, grandchildren and great-grandchildren. I did have ninety-two, but two have died. Seven of them are my children. The others are grandchildren and great-grandchildren. I can't begin to tell you how many are grandchildren and how many are great-grandchildren. That would be too much trouble, but there are ninety of them altogether."

The old man chuckled, while the daughter remarked: "That's all father does. He just sits on the porch and laughs."

"I'm as contented as if I was worth a million," the old man added. And then he said, "but I wish my pension was a little larger. The State allows me a pension for my part in the war of Texan independence. The amount is $12.50 a month. I have been told I was entitled to a land warrant, but I never got it."

"You must have begun voting pretty early, Mr. Cronea?"

"I cast my first vote for Andrew Jackson, the second time he ran. It was in 1824, wasn't it. Seems as if that was the year. I was living in Plaquemine at the time. They had a law that allowed only tax-payers to vote. When I went up, the judge of the election asked me if I was a tax-payer. I threw down a piece of money and said, 'Here is two-bits. Now I'm a tax-payer.' The judge raised some question. I knew him and knew that all of his property was in his wife's name. So I said to him, 'Judge, do you pay any taxes?' With that he said, 'Oh, come on; give us your vote.'"

The conversation turned again upon the ninety descendants. Mr. Cronea affirmed, with considerable pride, that all of them were born in three counties in Texas, and also that all of them are now living within the State for which he fought so valiantly. At a suggestion, four generations of the Cronea family were assembled upon the porch. The old gentleman, aged 87, sat at the head of the line. Next to him was his daughter, Mrs. Matilda Stough, aged 56. Mrs. Stough's daughter, Mrs. Artemis Wilryex, aged 34, sat beside her mother. Mrs. Wilryex was a widow until a week ago. She came over from a neighboring house leaning upon the arm of a new husband, and the pleasantries of her relatives prompted her to assume a rather abashed demeanor. The son of Mrs. Wilryex, Emile Andres, aged 10, sat on the edge of the porch near his great grandfather. As Mr. Cronea viewed the assembling of his clan, he remarked with a smile that it wasn't his fault there were not five generations instead of four lined up on the porch. He said he had three or four great-granddaughters who were old enough to be wives and mothers. While the four generations faced the artist, other members of the family stood about and offered more or less hilarious suggestions. Good humor is one of the strong traits of the Cronea descendants. They are all healthy, happy and handsome. Texas has no better people than the cabin-boy pirate and his ninety descendants.

Bolivar Peninsula is a queer place. This long, low-lying strip of land between Gulf and Bay possesses two physical phenomena which have puzzled scientific gentlemen. One of these is known as "the High Islands." The peninsula is quite level, being in the center only a little higher than along the beaches. Well toward the upper end of the peninsula the traveler comes to a collection of knolls, which rise sharply from the general level. These knolls can be seen from a great distance. In comparison with the almost dead level of sand and water on all sides of them they loom up like mountains. In reality the elevation is only 35 feet. Nothing like the soil of which the High Islands are composed can be found for many miles. This soil is a clay. On top of the knolls is a table-land several miles in extent. People have farms and live on the High Islands. Springs gush from the summits. Some of the springs are fresh water and some are salt. In one place a fresh spring and a salt spring come from the ground less than 2 feet apart. By digging down into the clay well water can be had. There are various theories as to how these High Islands came to be located away out on the flats of the Texas coast. From all of the conditions it would appear that a great section of a bluff country must have been cut off somewhere and carried down hundreds of miles and deposited on the Gulf front. A great glacier may be responsible for the strange freak.

Off Bolivar lie "the Oil Ponds." They are places in the Gulf where the breakers cease and the surf is at rest. In the very roughest weather there is some movement, but ordinarily the ponds are still, while all around them the ocean rolls. The natives of Bolivar say "the Oil Ponds" are what the name implies—collections of oil upon the surface of the water. But they do not call it oil. They call it sea wax. Within the memory of the oldest inhabitants of the peninsula the oil ponds have doubled in size. They seem to be growing. They cover many acres of water. Altogether they are fifteen miles long and two miles wide. The source of this collection of oil on the surface of the Gulf of Mexico, off Bolivar, is as mysterious as the origin of the High Islands. W. B. S.

THROUGH TEXAS.

The Story of What One Potato Did for Colorado City.

A Tomato and a Town Site—Midland's Inspiration—Rise and Fall of the Barons—Every Man His Own Irrigator—Abilene's Versatile Decade.

Special Correspondence of the Globe-Democrat.

ABILENE, TEX., August 29.—"Abilene!" Not a Winchester pops. Not a cowboy whoops. Queer ups and downs and ups again this Western Texas country has seen since 1882, just ten years ago. There are men in St. Louis and forty-nine other cities outside of Texas, who can shiver a little in August over investment memories of Abilene, of Sweetwater, of Colorado City, of Midland. What booms those were! The Texas and Pacific Railway had just gone through. The Comanche had just made room for the cowman. The man with a branding iron was bigger than the man with a bank. From the Brazos to the Colorado River was the prettiest country the tenderfoot ever saw.

Baird had been the town. When the railroad reached Baird it struck the great cattle trail leading from the Southern Texas ranges to Kansas and the North. The ranches for 250 miles did their trading at Baird. But the railroad came and the glory of Baird as the outfitting point departed westward. Abilene first, Sweetwater next, and then Colorado City bid and bid high for the favor of the cattle trade. Colorado City won, for she was the a brick thrown at random would hit at least one rich man, and in all probability carrom on another. In ten years a solid brick city, with 5000 inhabitants, was built on the high banks of the river. A $50,000 Court House wasn't good enough. Besides, it obstructed the view in the principal street. A new Court House was built, and the old one, constructed only two years before, was torn down. Corner lots in Colorado were held at $10,000, and some of them sold at that. Money was plentiful. Everybody had it or could borrow. A third party orator would have been satisfied

AN IRRIGATION PLANT AT MIDLAND.

gateway to the great pastureland of Texas, stretching 170 miles westward, from the Colorado River to the Pecos, and northward over the Staked Plains as far as the herds chose to roam.

Those were great days for cattlemen from 1881 almost to 1885. Never before had the steer been so profitable. Had the great seal of Texas been designed anew at that time it would have shown a long-horn rampant on the obverse and a long-horn couchant on the reverse. Prices of cattle went out of sight, and yet everybody wanted to buy. Lords and Earls came to Texas and exchanged good English gold for the title of cattle baron with all the name implied. Merchants and capitalists up North formed companies and sent high-salaried agents to take charge of their four-footed investments, "range count." And Colorado was the center and beneficiary of this tremendous activity in cows.

In 1884 there were more millionaires, present and prospective, on the streets of Colorado than in all the rest of Texas. It was said that with the "per capita." There were men with brand-new bank accounts who took it as a favor to be asked to indorse a note. There is a tradition to-day in Colorado about an old cattleman who spent the greater part of two days hunting for a stranger who wanted some paper indorsed. Pioneers who had started in business a few years previously with a branding iron found themselves worth hundreds of thousands of dollars.

In those flush days Colorado looked with scorn upon the farmer. In 1883 a German colony, under the leadership of a thrifty priest, settled upon a tract of land about eighty miles west of the cattlemen's capital. The place was called Marienfeld. A crop of wheat was raised, and the Germans with honest pride sent a bushel of it over to Colorado to be exhibited. The cattlemen were shocked. They said that sort of thing would ruin the country. They used harsh language about the grangers. But there came a time when the ranges around Colorado were overstocked. Then the bottom fell out of the cattle market. Prices went down and down.

In 1886 it took three steers to bring as many dollars as one had been worth three years before. Colorado had snubbed the farmer and she had warned the sheep herder. She had pinned her hope of prosperity to one thing—

ABILENE.

the cattle trade. The shrinkage on the $10,000 corner lots was something fearful to contemplate. A population of 5000 dwindled to 2000. Some were unfeeling enough to say that those who remained did so because they couldn't get away.

In this most trying period of Colorado's history came the discovery that all around Colorado was an agricultural country. One day somebody found an Irish potato sprouting through the ground just in front of the principal bank building. Colorado had eaten Irish potatoes at $2.50 a bushel and had never asked whence they came. This particular potato had rolled into the gutter in front of the bank and had taken a notion to grow. The man who made the discovery was the hero of the hour. After that everybody in town soon knew of the potato. Day by day for three months Colorado watched the progress of the potato's growth. It would have been worth a man's life to have disturbed it. Ex-millionaires were the most vigilant and interested observers of the volunteer experiment. Some of the children had to be told how potatoes reproduce. They had never seen the operation. The whole town became a farmers' club for the discussion of agricultural topics. Men who had loudest proclaimed the glorious character of a cowman's life and who had said they would rather commit suicide or shear sheep than handle a hoe, began to make gardens. One man scattered something less than half a ton of seed oats on unbroken prairie, scratched it well with a harrow and produced a fair crop.

That settled it. Colorado proclaimed far and wide that here was the place to farm. And the farmer, ignoring the snub of five years before, came, saw and conquered. The city has regained the population which went out with the cattle boom, but the personality is different. Colorado is still the center for the Western Texas cattle trade, but it is not that to the exclusion of agriculture, nor does it despise the shipment of 400 car loads of salt a month.

The potato which grew to such effect in front of Colorado's bank has its companion piece. An humble tomato plant developed in 1884 where Midland stands. For a week a party of excursionists, 150 strong, had been roaming over the State. Place after place had been visited, but nothing which quite filled the measure of desire was found. The excursionists were from Illinois and Iowa. They had money, and they wanted to start a town,

AT MIDLAND—JACK MILES; TIME, 48 SECONDS.

the beginning of which should be all their own. They came to what is now Midland, and found growing there this tomato plant. The dimensions seemed rather startling, but it is asserted that the vine was 9 feet high and spread out 7 feet in diameter. This vine was loaded with tomatoes from top to bottom. It settled the minds of the excursionists, who said, "Here we rest, build a town and sell corner lots to our friends." Six hours after the excursionists set eyes on the tomato plant the town company had been organized. The sale of lots followed. Midland has 1500 people who do a

and discovered after all that her territory was much better suited for sheep than for steers. The flock-masters, usually the most despised of men in a cow country, were received with open arms by Abilene. They and their flocks overran the Abilene country,

BRANDING CATTLE.

business of $1,500,000 a year with the ranch owners of the Staked Plains. The town is surrounded by gardens of from one to ten acres. Each garden has its well, its windmill and storage pond, called "tank," for water. This is the individual system of irrigation. It comes pretty near reaching perfection at Midland. The little orchards, vineyards and gardens give results which almost parallel and help to make credible the tomato plant story. The product is from $100 to $300 an acre. On these little tracts the yield has been as much as 600 bushels of sweet potatoes and 800 bushels of onions to the acre. The ranch trade takes all the sweet potatoes at 2c a pound and the onions at 3c and 4c a pound. These "ten-acres-enough" irrigators have begun to experiment in other directions than vegetables. They have tried prunes and raisin grapes on a small scale, and they think they can compete with California, with the advantage of half of the distance and less freight rates. What rain falls on this lower end of the Staked Plains country comes in summer for the most part. It is about 20 inches. That means a dry climate where the man with the rasping cough, the transparent skin and the flushed cheek may prolong his days and substitute moderate good health for short-lived misery.

Abilene in ten years ran the gamut of experience. She won and lost the supremacy as the outfitting point for the cattle trade. As this drifted westward Abilene "lit on her feet,"

and before the Southwest generally had realized the change Abilene had become the principal wool market of Texas. The shipments of wool at this point climbed to 8,000,000 pounds in a year. The Northern shepherd must remember that this is a country where the wool is taken off twice a year by many sheep growers.

IN THE CATTLE PENS AT COLORADO.

Abilene is nothing if not versatile. While the sheep industry flourished she remembered the fate of her cattle trade and she also recognized that sheep can travel. Without waiting for potatoes to grow in front of her banks she held an agricultural fair. An agricultural fair in Western Texas in 1884! It paralyzed the natives. Then a Board of Trade was organized. Roads were laid out, all leading to

Abilene of course. Ten or fifteen bridges were built. Soon the whole face of the country was changed. There wasn't anything left to make the visiting cowboy feel at home except the names of the creeks, such, for instance, as the Jim Ned, the Bull Wagon and like examples of range nomenclature. For several years Abilene carried off the sweepstakes premium for her agricultural exhibit in competition with thirty or forty other counties at the State Fair. And now there are 7000 people in Abilene. They tell about their wheat and their oats shipments. Several thousand farms have been opened up in the county. Abilene begins to have the airs of a long-settled and seriously respectable city. She has manufactories of various kinds, some possibilities in iron and coal deposits, a solid, well-balanced trade of numerous lines. And yet but ten short years ago what a riproaring town Abilene was! W. B. S.

THROUGH TEXAS.

The Lost Mine and the Ancient Church on the Rio Grande.

A Padre's Story—Web Flanagan on Living Issues—Cosmopolitan El Paso—A Tariff that Did Not Prohibit.

Special Correspondence of the Globe-Democrat.

EL PASO, TEX., September 3.—Tourists who stop in El Paso on the way to the City of Mexico or California do not fail to visit the ancient church at Juarez. Electric cars cross the Rio Grande. The thirty seconds' stop for the customs officer to walk through the car is only a pleasant episode. While the forms against smuggling are being complied with the stranger has his choice of two methods of amusement. He can speculate on the ease with which he has evaded the laws of his country, or he can look innocently out of the car window upon the lower-class Mexicans bathing *in puris naturalibus* along the banks below.

The old church on the square at Juarez is in every guide book. It is the first introduction to ancient Mexico. It has been much written about. People from Maine to Oregon have dropped their nickels in the slot "for the repair of the church." But not many became sufficiently well acquainted with the good padre to hear "the story of the lost mine." Every locality where precious metals have been found has its "lost mine." El Paso County is not exceptional. Tradition links this particular lost mine with the ancient church. At the corner of the edifice, to the left of the main entrance, is a tower. The door is usually kept padlocked. Visitors are free to enter the church and look at the curiously jointed wooden ceiling, the pulpit with its eccentric stair on one side, the confessional wholly unlike those seen in Catholic churches in the United States, and the Madonna-like face of Our Lady of Guadalupe. Even the great wooden cross, on which is hung a ghastly form for the crucifixion procession once a year, is exhibited, but the tower is closed. Those who are permitted by special favor to pass the door find a stairway of logs, the ends of which overlap and form the axis of the circling steps without any other

MEXICAN SUBURB OF EL PASO.

support. At the top of this freak in architecture there is a small room with outlooks through the heavy walls. And from this tower the way leads to the lost mine. The church itself is on an elevation. The tower gives a view over the flat tops of the one-story houses. In the distance can be seen the tion and look through a certain window in the tower and in a line with certain natural landmarks. If the conditions are fully com-

IN THE OLD CHURCH AT JUAREZ.

Franklin Mountains, and there is the lost mine. According to the tradition one must stand in a certain posi- plied with the vision will rest on the exact location of the lost mine. But where is the place to stand, which is the window, and what are the landmarks? The padre shakes his head. He would like to know himself.

By the tradition this mine was worked before the Spanish conquest. It was very rich. From it the natives along the Rio Grande obtained the massive gold ornaments which they wore when the Spaniards came. In the early history of the church many of these golden ornaments were laid upon the altar. But there came a long and stubborn war with the conquerors. Incursions of Apaches and Comanches made the mountains unhealthy. Afterwards the Pueblo rebellion engrossed attention, and still later was the American invasion. Amid exciting scenes the natives lost their mine. Their descendants have nothing except the tradition of the church tower and window to guide them to it. And not one of them seems to care to look for the landmarks. They fold their scrapes about them and stand beside the adobe in poverty all of their lives rather than climb to the top of the tower and look. The restless American is the only one who tries to solve the riddle. He visits the tower, ponders long on the landscape, goes forth to search, and never finds the mine.

"There is the very kindest feeling here with Mexico," said Col. Web Flanagan, Collector of the Port of El Paso, in reply to a question. "The future of our trade relations is very bright. The re-election of President Diaz means progress, and the same may be said of Gov. Armido, just elected Governor of Chihuahua."

The friendliness is something more than diplomatic. Mexicans live in El Paso; Americans do business in Juarez. The Mexicans cut grain with a sickle and tread it out by driving burros in a circle on the American side of the river. An American clears $13,000 to $15,000 a year from a vineyard on the Mexican side of the Rio. This is a happy state of affairs. The only thing that is holding El Paso back is the need of more water for irrigation. The development of the valley has outgrown the Rio Grande. Only the other day the authorities on the Mexican side issued an order directing that the water be turned from the Mexican ditches into the river two days in the week, in order that the poor people on the American side might save their crops. A great international dam, which will store the water in time of surplus for time of need, will double the population and production of the valley in two years. El Paso already has the dam on paper.

El Paso is cosmopolitan. Jay Gould, in search of health, spent four or five weeks here last spring. This was the one place where he could leave his private car and walk about like a plain every-day American citizen. No committee intruded upon him. People didn't turn around and look after him or make remarks about him in his hearing, or treat him as a museum freak at large. He took occasion, before his departure, to remark upon this admirable characteristic of the El Paso peo-

NEXT TO GODLINESS.

ple, and to explain that he had prolonged his stay because of it.

The customs revenue at El Paso has reached $675,000. Last year it was $550,000; the year before that, $50,000. The increase is the tariff put upon ore from Mexico. Ninety per cent of the revenue collected at El Paso is from the ore importation. From twenty to twenty-five car-loads of silver-lead ore comes from Mexico across the Rio Grande daily. It was argued when the duty was put on that it would be prohibition; that smelters would be moved to Mexico and the importations would cease. Instead of that, the ore keeps coming. miner has the ore to sell and he goes on shipping and paying the tariff that amounts to a division of the Mexican miner's profits with the United States Government. The smelters in this region are bound to have the Mexican ore for fluxing. They pay a little more for this ore than they did before the tariff was put on and make up for it by charging more for smelting. Thus the burden distributes itself and the Mexican ores keep coming. The Mexican miner gets less for his ore; the smelter charges more for smelting; the Government of the United States adds half a million a year to its revenue. The increase

MEXICAN WINE VATS.

THE SAMPLING WORKS.

El Paso, instead of losing business for the smelters she had, feels confident she could keep two more smelters busy. This tariff legislation has a way of confounding the prophets occasionally. Importations of ore have increased instead of diminished since the imposition of the duty. The Mexican has already been enough to pay for the handsome new Custom House into which Collector Flanagan has just moved, and which the Treasury agents say has no superior anywhere in Federal architecture.

The Mexicans protested mightily against the tariff put on their ore by the United

States. Yet it turned out to be one of the best things that ever happened to that country. It inspired the idea of building smelters south of the Rio Grande. The smelters on this side didn't stop on account of the tariff. They simply split the difference—took part of it from the price paid to the Mexican miner and added the other part to the charge upon the American miner for smelting. But other smelters were built in Mexico. Before the tariff was put on the Mexicans were taking out twenty tons of ore for every ton shipped. On account of the high transportation charges, they couldn't afford to send the nineteen tons to the American market. With smelters of their own close at hand, the Mexicans are working up the ore formerly thrown upon the dump.

Mr. F. W. Edelsten, formerly Government assayer at El Paso, and now at the head of the El Paso Sampling Works, speaking of the radical change of mining conditions in Mexico, said: "I don't think there is any question that the silver product of Mexico this year will exceed that of the United States. Last year the silver product of this country was $58,000,000. Mexico was $11,000,000 behind. Last year, on the 1st of January, there wasn't a single smelter of any magnitude in Mexico. If Mexico was only $11,000,000 below the United States then what can she do when the nineteen tons out of twenty, which was formerly thrown away, is reduced, as is now the case?"

"Is silver production increasing in the United States?"

THE SMELTER.

AN APIARY IN THE ALFALFA COUNTRY.

"I doubt very much if the product of this country will reach $58,000,000 this year."

"What about Mexico's future?"

"Mexico is the greatest silver country in the world. You have heard of the Sierra Mojada—the wet mountain? That is proving to be the greatest lead carbonate deposit in the world. allow a company to work them on shares. It costs the company only $3 a ton for the actual mining. The ore is piled up and divided evenly. That brings the cost to the company $6 a ton. This ore is worth $28 a ton. From this margin the company has already made a great fortune. About half of the ore now com-

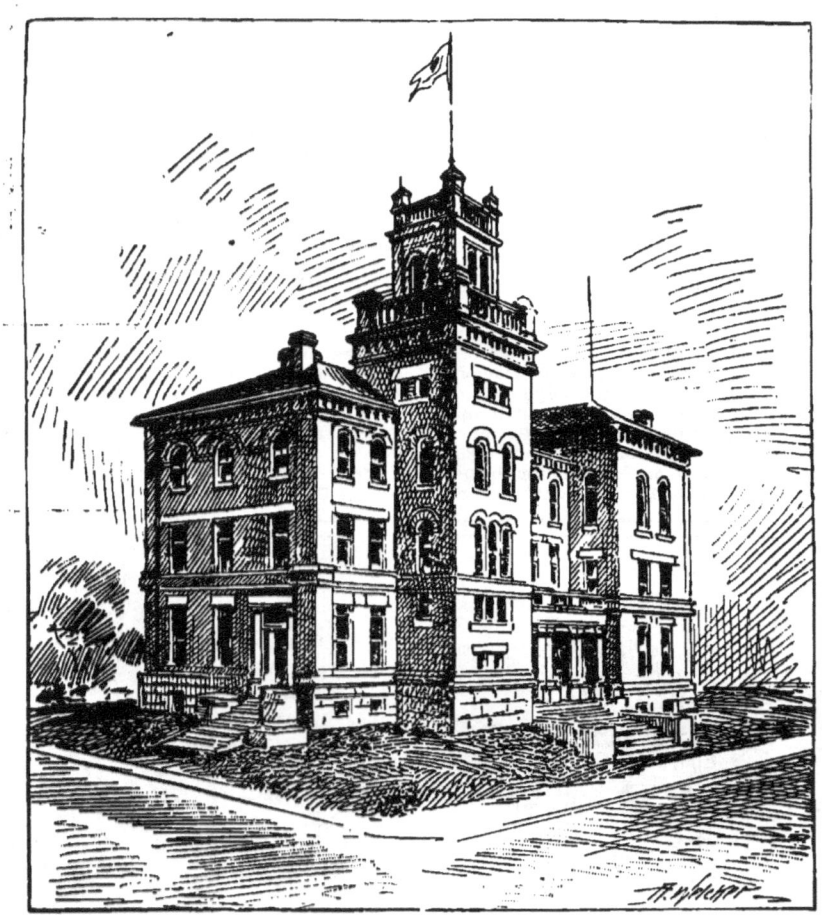

EL PASO'S NEW CUSTOM HOUSE.

Leadville isn't a marker. Sierra Mojada is a great mountain. They put in tunnels anywhere from 60 to 80 feet and get ore. There are chambers from which the ore bodies have been taken, large enough to hold the St. Louis Exposition building. The ore goes 20 ounces of silver and 25 per cent lead. The great deposits are owned by Mexicans, who ing to El Paso is from the Sierra Mojada. It is especially desirable for mixing with American ores in smelting."

Ore sampling comes very near reaching perfection at El Paso. Ore sells in car-load lots on the sampling certificate, just as wheat changes hands with its grade determined by the inspector's visit. But the ore sampling is more responsible than the grain inspecting. If the ore falls short of the sampling certificate in value, the difference must be made up by the sampler, not by the former owner of the ore. A random grab at a car-load of ore might show 100 ounces of silver or 10 ounces of silver to the ton. Hence the necessity for the most complete mixing and averaging of values. The car-load of ore goes into an automatic machine which mixes it and lets out one-tenth of it. That machine enables four men to do what would require twenty without it. The one-tenth of a car-load is cut down to four wheelbarrow loads by shoveling. The four wheelbarrow loads go through small rolls reducing the ore to gravel. One-fourth of this is taken and quartered to 50 pounds. The 50 pounds is put through a grinder, which further mixes it and cuts down the sample to half a shovel. That goes to a table which must first be carefully cleaned with brick-dust. This cleaning is more necessary than it looks. If the previous sample has been high-grade it may leave enough metal on the table, but for the cleaning, to make a difference of 100 ounces to the ton. Out of the final mixing and dividing on the table a half ounce of ore is taken. and from that the assayer determines the amount of gold, silver and lead in the whole car-load of ore. And on the assayer's verdict from the half-ounce assay the ore changes hands by the car-load. Nine times the ore is mixed and divided in rapidly reducing amounts until one-tenth of an ounce is fairly representative of the entire car-load.

Grain men understand very well the elevator art of adding to and taking from, so as to improve the grade. In the sampling business there is something akin to this. When the amount of lead falls below a certain percentage, 5, the smelters do not allow anything for it. The sampling may show 4 per cent of lead, and if the ore be left as it is the 4 per cent of lead is entirely lost to the miner. It is a feature of the sampling business, in such cases, to add from rich lead, one kept in stock, enough to carry the whole car-load to 5 per cent, and thus the value of the 4 per cent of lead is gained to the miner. By a similar rule the smelter does not allow for the gold in the ore if it runs below one-tenth of an ounce. There may be $1.80 worth of gold in the ore, but it is lost to the miner if the ore is passed along to the smelter unchanged. It is part of the sampling business in that event to add 10c worth of gold, bringing the value up to $1.90, and getting that out of the smelter. In the assay office at El Paso there is a little fragment of ore something larger than a thumb nail. It is from the Santa Margarita. A St. Louis boy, Mr. Heckelman, owned the mine, but he fell sick, and under the rigid mining law of Mexico he could not hold it without performing a certain amount of work. Santa Margarita passed into the possession of a Mexican. The other day the new owner came into El Paso with two little sacks of ore. The contents netted him $10,000. If he had had a ton it would have been worth $104,000.

W. B. S.

THROUGH TEXAS.

The Days of Elephants and Three-Toed Horses on the Staked Plains.

A Geological Freak—The White Sand Hills—Forests of Trees Shin High—The Seven Wells—Palo Duro's Wonder.

Special Correspondence of the Globe-Democrat.

BEYOND THE BRAZOS, TEX., September 4.— This is not the brand new country which some people suppose it is. These hills of Western Texas have their traditions of hidden wealth, once found, but lost. The same kind of stories that old settlers in the Ozarks of Missouri tell are current here—about Spaniards who carried off bullion by the burro load. In the beautiful Arbuckle Mountains of the Indian Territory there are abandoned mines and the ruins of an abandoned town which looks as if a couple of centuries or more may have passed since occupation. Traces of silver are found in a dozen counties of Texas between the Brazos and the Colorado. From the car window one can read in flaming letters:

```
         OLDEN,
FUTURE GOLD AND SILVER MINING
         CITY OF TEXAS.
```

Here a small smelter has been built in the woods. Web Flanagan says the prospectors have found ore which assays $16 of silver to the ton. But so far no bonanzas have been found. If the Spaniards got out great wealth, they either exhausted the deposits or left no pointers for future generations. That they roamed over Western Texas there is abundant evidence. The trail of Coronado has been discovered upon the Staked Plain. In the Yellow Horse Canyon of the Upper Panhandle there was uncovered a complete suit of Spanish armor. The Big Spring, in Howard County, was a camping place for white men long before the day of the oldest settler. A few years ago a cloud burst just above the spring and washed it out. In the debris, when the waters subsided, were picked up many old flint-lock musket barrels and some patterns of firearms wholly unknown in later days.

The Indian population of Texas must have been very large at some remote period. Around the water holes and springs of the timbered portions of the State the traces of Indian settlements are general. Before white settlers came in and gathered them up, the metales on which the Indian women ground the corn, just as the Mexicans do to-day, could be seen in great numbers wherever there was living water. Arrow-heads were very numerous. Texas, however, has few mounds. Her Indians were not of that class. They were more like the cave dwellers. In the Guada-
think the tract is the bed of an ancient fresh water lake. Others believe it to be the former course of the Pecos River, which now flows swiftly through a channel forty miles further west. The White Sand Hills skirt the western edge of the Staked Plain and cross into New Mexico. In winter this freak is the most desolate strip on earth, outside of Death Valley and the Sahara. The hills shift and drift with the winds, and are for the most part bare of vegetation. But in May and June the surface is a vast flower bed, brilliant and fascinating. The floral carpet gives way later to tall sedge grass. At a glance this appears to be the dryest spot on the globe. A trip among the hills shows the strip to be unusually well

SIGNAL MOUNTAIN.

loupe and Diabolo mountains are many caverns; and nearly all of them show signs of Indian occupation. Some were used for burial places. Others were carefully prepared for purposes of defense. Still others were warehouses in which provisions in great quantities were stored.

There were elephants in Texas—plenty of them—in the early days. Bones and teeth have been dug up at Wild Horse Spring. From these it is evident that the elephant roamed in Howard County, 2400 feet above the sea level and upon the Great Staked Plain.

Lying between the Great Staked Plain and the Pecos, is a geological freak. It is called "the White Sand Hills." This curious body of land is 150 miles long, and from five to thirty miles wide. Scientific men who have seen it hold diverse theories as to how it came into existence. The level of White Sand Hills is 500 feet below the Staked Plain. Some
watered. Scattered among the sand dunes are hundreds of small ponds, which contain the purest water to be found in Texas. Around the ponds grows most luxuriant vegetation. It consists chiefly of tule grass and tall reeds. Scattered through the hills are forests of shin oaks. Approaching one of these forests, the traveler might imagine himself in Lilliput. The shin oak tree grows from 6 inches to a foot high. It usually bears, for its size, a tremendous crop of fairly large acorns. In the sand heaps are sometimes found the trunks of trees from 18 inches to 2 feet in diameter. They have the bark on and are in a fair state of preservation, but they evidently belong to past ages. Nothing larger than the shin oak and the mesquite brush now grows in the White Sand Hills. The mast is abundant enough to stock the big Fort Worth packery, which eats up a hog a minute when it can get them. But this mast serves at present to maintain a great variety

of wild animal life. The jack rabbit is the mastodon of the shin oak forests. He can skip about and look over the tops of the trees without half trying. Molly Cotton-tail, first cousin to Jack Rabbit, is numerous. There is a peculiar little ground squirrel which industriously gathers the acorns and stores them in a hole under a mesquite bush. Then comes along the peccary, or javalina, the wild hog of Texas, industriously digs a larger and deeper hole under the same mesquite bush and eats the squirrel's acorns, passing on with a snort of defiance to capital both alien and domestic. Black tail deer, an occasional skunk and the yelping coyote make up the wild animal life of this queer region.

Horses, cattle and civilized hogs live in the White Sand Hills and do well. The cowboys say that the white sand gets hot enough on a summer day to heat water. They claim to take the coffee pot from the fire and set it on the sand to hurry the boiling. They tell a story of two shepherds toiling through the White Sand Hills with flocks of sheep. One was driving close to the railroad track. The other was half a mile away. A train rattled by at the rate of twenty-five miles an hour,

A RANCH OF RAILROAD TIES.

LATE OWNERS OF THE STAKED PLAINS.

On the rear platform of the sleeper sat a fat old fellow in his shirt sleeves. He had a glass of something in one hand and a palm leaf fan in the other. The sight turned the head of the shepherd by the track. He left his flock and waded half a mile through the sand to the other shepherd just for the purpose of asking him if he had "seen that." And then the two took turns in abusing with all of the picturesque and expressive language they could remember a man whom neither had ever met and whose only crime was being comfortable. That is human nature in the White Sand Hills of Texas and in the third party.

siderable strength. The water comes in at one side and passes out through the other. Its direction is toward the Pecos River. One theory advanced in explanation of these wells is that a roof of a great cavern through which an underground river passes has dropped down in places.

In digging wells in the Sand Hills many bones are found. They are remains of mastodons, bear, mountain lions, elephants and other large animals not now found in Texas. The White Sand Hills country seems to be very rich in these things, and it is a field which has scarcely been touched.

A strange formation is found in the Seven

WALLS OF THE PALO DURO.

The underground water supply of the White Sand Hills is another of the surprises of this region. For well digging the conditions seem to be most forbidding. Yet good water is found at depths varying from the grass roots to 30 feet. And when the flow is struck it is practically inexhaustible. There seems to be some underground communication with the Pecos. Either that is the case or else the whole Sand Hills strip is over a river which flows slowly through the sand.

Fifteen miles south of the place where the White Sand Hills come to an end is an isolated peak known as Castle Mountain. Near the mountain is a series of natural wells. Water does not rise to the surface and flow, but in all of the wells there is a current of con-

Wells of Mitchell County. That is in this same interesting region of Western Texas. At the junction of two creeks is a bed of friable gray sandstone mixed with coarse gravel. Water passing over the ledge has worn away a part of it, and has created a fall of 30 feet. The loose gravel carried round and round in the eddies has gradually bored holes in the sandstone. These holes are from 3 to 6 feet wide, circular, and from 50 to 100 feet deep. There are from fifteen to twenty of them, all filled with fresh water. By the long continued churning of the gravel they have been made jug-shaped or cistern-like, and in some instances the wall dividing two wells has been cut through. This must have been a favorite watering place with the buffalo. In the solid rock is cut a deep trail down to the water. And where the descent is steepest the foot-marks are over 6 inches deep, showing that every animal passing there put its foot exactly in the spot occupied by those which had preceded it.

In the thrilling Indian and border stories of twenty years ago figured a chasm of the plain. Sometimes the description was of a herd of buffalo stampeding toward the brink, and suddenly plunging downward a thousand feet to wholesale death. Occasionally the able pen of the romancer pictured similar de- 1500 feet deep. In places they fall sheer; in other places they are not quite so abrupt. But for sixty miles there is only one crossing of the canyon for loaded wagons. You drive over a treeless, boundless plain, the short, soft buffalo grass deadening sound and easing jolts. There is no previous indication of the chasm. The break in the surface is not noticeable until the horses are within a few feet of the edge. Leaning over, you look down upon a strange scene. There is a wall at your feet and another from half a mile to two miles opposite. Between these walls, at the base, is river, meadow, pine forest, water-

THE WATERFALL OF PALO DURO.

struction of Indians in a fight with the ever-victorious "long guns." Again fancy took the lonely scout to the brink of the precipice, and showed his faithful stud rearing backward from the edge of the abyss. This chasm on the plain was the favorite spot for the crisis of the plot. People of the age of discretion who glanced over the Indian stories of twenty years ago gave no more credence to the chasm than they did to the rest of the marvels. But the chasm was and is a fact. It can be visited to-day by those who do not shrink from a fifteen or twenty miles drive across the plain from any one of half a dozen railroad stations in the Panhandle of Texas. The chasm is nearly 100 miles long. Its course is from northwest to southeast. The precipices are from 300 to fall, all combined. But the tops of the tallest pines come nowhere near the level of the plain. This is the Palo Duro canyon. It is as much a curiosity in its way as the Big Trees of Calaveras, the Yellowstone Park or the Grand Canyon. In some parts of its sixty or eighty miles course the Palo Duro is wild and rugged. In others it broadens until there is room for pastures as well as for forests. From the edge above, the river below looks like an insignificant brook. But small as it appears, it is one of the main tributaries of the Red River, and it comes all of the way from the mountains.

In the walls of the Palo Duro canyon the scientists read the beginning of things. In the region about they are having a grand round-up of fossils this summer. From one bed have been resurrected seven kinds of horses. Some of them had three toes and were no larger than dogs. Of camels, rhinoceroses and mastodons there are two kinds each in this great aggregation of bones. Cormorants were uncovered in great variety. More horses, three species of mastodons, camels, magalonyx and three kinds of land turtles have been dug up within a few weeks in another locality. One of these tortoises is a monster. He is as large as the largest turtles found along the Gulf coast, measuring more than 3 feet across the shell. Along Tulle canyon, a branch of the great Palo Duro, is found the highest elevation of the Staked Plain, and there is located the greatest show on earth in fossils. In one bed can be seen the bones of elephants, horses, camels, tortoises and numerous small animals. Scattered among the bones are shells, and 400 feet below in the bottom of the canyon these same kinds of shells are found alive in the water. All of the discoveries made by the scientists in this midsummer exploration were not fossilized. In springs and creeks outside of Texas there is occasionally seen a repulsive little animal called a water-dog. It is cold, slimy and smooth-skinned. On the Staked Plains the water-dogs are at home. In the lakes they are as thick as tadpoles in a frog pond, and when a rain storm comes these reptiles leave the lakes and crawl in all directions. They are innumerable. They make themselves as disagreeable as the frogs did in Egypt. W. B. S.

THROUGH TEXAS.

A Visit to Senora Candelaria, Heroine of the Alamo—The Brave Spanish Woman in Whose Arms Bowie was Butchered—Her Story of How David Crockett and His Followers Met Death.

"Thermopylæ had Her Messenger of Defeat, but the Alamo had None."

Skeptical Tom Rife—Housekeeping at the Age of 107—The Missions—How Indians were Converted—"Santone's" Fifty Years of Revolutions.

Special correspondence of the Globe-Democrat.

SAN ANTONIO, TEX., September 6.—"Over the San Pedro," the San Antonian says. "Over the San Pedro" is the Mexican market. "Over the San Pedro" is everything Mexican. "Over the San Pedro" Senora Candelaria lives. The San Pedro comes bubbling up from the bowels of the earth in three great springs a little way out of San Antonio. So much of it as isn't led off into irrigating ditches, wriggles its way through the most densely settled part of the city. By common consent the San Pedro has come to be the dividing line between American San Antonio and Mexican San Antonio. And by general usage "over the San Pedro" now stands for the Mexican San Antonio.

"Senora Candelaria," the San Antonian said, "lives over the San Pedro." He didn't seem to think it was necessary to add anything more definite. And so "over the San Pedro" the way was taken. One needs to have his eyes open or he will get "over the San Pedro" without knowing it. The stream comes stealing down among the houses and under sidewalks and bridge without any noise or fuss. It is as mild-mannered as the Mexi-

THE ALAMO.

cans have been in later years before the aggressive, pushing American, who now calls his San Antonio the San Antonio and recognizes the Mexican San Antonio as only "over the San Pedro." The stream is crossed. The house fronts become a little more distinctively Mexican. Through the open doors is heard an unfamiliar language, soft and sibilant. At a corner where the beer kegs smell or stale by any other name, the inquiry is made once more for Senora Candelaria. And straightway a dark-skinned Mexican in a high hat leaves the group of his fellows and leads the way down a side street. He stops at a narrow passage between two houses, looks back and passes in. He turns a corner, crosses a little court-yard, turns another corner, enters a little house which stands by itself, goes through a kitchen such as might do for children to play at house-keeping, and stops on the threshold of another little room. The next moment he is explaining to the senora sitting in her low rocking chair that these senores have come all the way from St. Louis to see her. The withered hand which gave Bowie his last sup of water ere the bayonets pierced him on his sick bed, is held out in welcome. The dimmed eyes which saw David Crockett fall in front of the Alamo, are turned upon the visitors. The ears which heard Travis appeal to his fellow Texans to "die with him" listened to the explanation of the guide.

One hundred and seven years old, Senora Candelaria is the only survivor of the Alamo. Bowie was sick with the typhoid fever when Santa Anna came with his army to take San Antonio. The Americans retreated to the old church of the Alamo, and fortified themselves there for desperate defense. Bowie had his cot carried in. There Senora Candelaria went to nurse the sick man, and there she remained through the desperate struggle which ended only when every man of the 172 Americans was dead.

The senora speaks a little English. When she knew that the story of the Alamo was wanted in all its thrilling details from her own lips she sent for her grandson, a trim, handsome young man, to act as interpreter.

In 1835 Santa Anna set aside republican forms of government in Mexico. He ignored the Constitution. He ordered the militia reduced to a minimum and disarmed. That furnished the Americans in Texas their formal grounds for revolt. They raised an army, and after desperate fighting took San Antonio, forcing surrender of the Mexican troops. Then they disbanded and went home, all save a small body of men left under arms at San Antonio. Politics took the place of war. A "consultation" of Americans was held and a provisional government was organized. Santa Anna started from Mexico with an army to crush the rebellion. And when he approached San Antonio the little body of Americans, instead of retreating, marched into the Alamo church. They took with them twenty or thirty beeves. They tore down Mexican huts and carried the wood inside for cooking. To every man was assigned his place on the walls for defense. David Crockett and his twelve Tennesseeans were given the main entrance to hold. Santa Anna reached the suburbs of San Antonio.

A SAN ANTONIO RIVER SCENE.

Leaning forward, speaking rapidly, using her hands to emphasize her description, the little senora told the story which has no parallel in history save, perhaps, Thermopylæ. Again and again the grandson was obliged to check the torrent of language that he might interpret. Fifty-six years ago the Alamo fell, but the event is as of yesterday in Senora Candelaria's memory.

He had 4000 men. He waited eight days for Tolsa to join him with 2000 more. That made an army of 6000 to capture an old church held by 172 Texans. Santa Anna sent a couple of officers with a white flag demanding surrender. Travis replied defiantly with a shot from the cannon which had been dragged into the church and hoisted into the tower.

"We were expecting the attack every day," said the senora, "and one morning at 4 o'clock it came. We heard the drums and the bugles, and then the firing began. It was all over by 9 o'clock." She held up her hands and shook her head.

The Mexicans assaulted in four columns. They were close up to the walls before the Texans made any response. They were even mounting the ladders when flames shot out from every part of the church and court. Those of the attacking party who did not fall before the fearful volley were struck upon the head with clubbed muskets and thrown down the ladders. The Texans had heaped up bags of sand breast high at the doors. They had protected themselves in a similar manner on the walls. Every time a Texan's rifle cracked a Mexican's life went out.

"I have never seen men die before with the indifference of these Mexicans," said a European officer under Maximilian upon one occasion. It was this characteristic of the Mexican soldier which sealed the fate of the defenders of the Alamo. Repeatedly the ladders were cleared and the ground below was covered with dead and dying, but onward moved those attacking columns. And finally, perhaps because of the exhaustion of the defenders, perhaps because ammunition temporarily failed, one of the assaulting parties was able to gain a footing on a corner of the fort.

Crockett died in front of the main entrance. Tradition has it that he was almost covered with the bodies of Mexicans who fell at his hands. Senora Candelaria says this is not true. Just at the left, as one passes in at the main door of the church, is a little corner room walled off from the main portion of the church. In that room the senora was nursing the dying Bowie, inventor of the knife which bears his name. Through the door of this room she saw David Crockett come forward to the main entrance as an assaulting column approached. She saw him leap upon the barricade of sand bags as if to meet death half way, and she saw him fall before one of the first volleys. There were others who fought behind the barricade to the last. They used their rifles as long as the enemy's distance gave them time to load. Then with clubbed guns they struck down the Mexicans as often as they tried to climb over the sand bags. And when some of the Mexicans had gained the interior the Texans cut them down with their knives. At last the Mexicans wheeled a cannon in front of that barricade of sand bags, charged it with grape and canister and fired it point-blank through the main entrance. They repeated this and then they entered. Fifteen dead Texans lay on one side of the sand bags and forty-two dead Mexicans on the other side.

"Bowie," said Senora Candelaria, "was too sick to do any fighting. He had the typhoid fever. When the Mexicans came in they killed him. After that I tried to keep them from mutilating the body. Other Mexican soldiers came in. I pretended to be giving Bowie a cup of water. I held his head in my arms so."

The senora raised her arms and went through the pantomime.

"I told them," she continued, "that Bowie was dying and I tried to keep them off. One of them thrust his bayonet toward Bowie. He struck me and made this."

The senora raised her chin and pointed to the deep scar which over half a century had failed to wipe out. She was pushed over by the force of the thrust, and as she lay there bleeding she saw the Mexican soldiers plunge

SENORA CANDELARIA AT 107.

their bayonets into Col. Bowie's body, raise it high in air above their heads and hold it there while the blood ran down their guns and over their clothes.

In most battles the wounded exceed the dead, four or five to one. At the Alamo the proportions were reversed. Within the church there were no wounded when the fighting ceased. Every Texan was dead. The night before the morning of the assault one Texan left the Alamo. His name was Rose. He leaped down from the wall and made his way out of the city and into the country. His story was that every one of the 172 comrades he left behind deliberately chose death. Travis, as Rose told it, called the band together and said there was no longer any hope of re-enforcements.

"We must die," were his words. "Three modes are presented to us. Let us choose that by which we may best serve our country. Shall we surrender and be shot without taking the life of a single enemy? Shall we try to cut our way out through Mexican ranks and be butchered before we can kill twenty of our adversaries? I am opposed to either of those methods. Let us resolve to withstand our adversaries to the last, and at each advance to kill as many of them as possible. And when at last they storm our fortress let us kill them as they come; kill them as they scale our wall; kill them as they leap within; kill them as they raise their weapons and as they use them; kill them as they kill our companions, and continue to kill as long as one of us shall remain alive."

And that impassioned appeal was followed to the letter. Travis gave to every man his choice of adopting this course or attempting to escape.

"Should any man prefer to surrender or to attempt an escape, he is at liberty to do so," Travis said. Rose looked at the walls and then around him. He saw Crockett leaning over Bowie's cot and talking in low, earnest tones. Bowie saw Rose and said quietly, "You seem not to be willing to die with us, Rose."

Rose replied, "No, I am not prepared to die, and shall not do so if I can help it."

Then Crockett took up the conversation and said: "You may as well conclude to die with us, old man; there is no escape."

No tinge of reproach was in the tones. All were as men already in the shadow. Rose climbed slowly to the top of the wall. He

"OVER THE SAN PEDRO."

"My choice," said the commander, "is to stay in the fort and die for my country, fighting as long as breath shall remain in my body."

He drew a mark down the front of the line and said: "I now want every man who is determined to stay here and die with me to cross this. Who will be the first?"

Tapley Holland stepped forward the next instant, saying, "I am ready to die for my country." And every man but Rose followed.

Col. Bowie heard and saw what was going on. Raising himself on his elbow he said; "Boys, I am not able to come to you, but I wish some of you would be so kind as to move my cot over there." Four men lifted the cot and placed it on the die-but-never-surrender side. Several others who were sick followed Bowie's example.

looked down. The men were going about arranging everything for the final struggle. None of them looked at him or spoke. Rose dropped on the outside, crawled along the ground, sought the deepest shadows, forded the river and reached the outskirts of the city. He was not far away when the deep boom told him that the cannonading had been resumed.

How many Mexicans fell at the Alamo? There is only Mexican authority for it, but the number of their dead is given as 521 and the wounded as 300. Another Mexican report of the battle is that 2,000 were killed. In one of these reports it is stated that the dead Mexicans were generally shot in the head, and that few of the wounds inflicted were below the neck and shoulders.

"After the battle," said the senora, "I begged from the officers the body of Col.

Bowie. They would not let me have it. All of the Americans were taken out on the plaza burned the rest of the day till sundown. After that what was left of the bones was buried

IN FRONT OF THE ALAMO.

and piled up, first a lot of wood and then a lot of bodies; more wood and more bodies. When all were in a heap, the wood was fired. It near a corner of the plaza. I wanted to give Col. Bowie burial, but he was burned with the others.''

The senora makes no mistake in her age. She says she is 107. And when asked the year of her birth she answers, without a moment's hesitation, "In November, 1785." She is strong, she says—all but the eyes. Vision has been failing now for two or three years. But the hearing is right. In her little home she does her own work, and is only unhappy when her son insists that she shall leave some of her household duties to others.

"My father," explained the grandson, "doesn't want her to do her washing, but she will steal off to the back of the houses and hide from him to wash her own clothes. She likes nothing better than to have Gen. Stanley, with whom she is well acquainted, come here and let her cook a Mexican dinner for him."

TELLING THE STORY.

While the young man spoke the old lady nodded and laughed, as if she partly understood what he was saying. To all Americans she is known as the Senora Candelaria.

"Candelaria," she said, "is not my real name. I assumed that in going among the Americans, with whom I sympathized. My name from my parents was Andrae Castanon. My father was a Spanish officer of rank in Cuba. My mother was of Mexico. I was born in Laredo on St. Andrew's day, 1785. At the time of the troubles here between the Americans and the Mexicans I had money and property. I was rich. My sympathies were with the Americans. I nursed the American soldiers when they were sick and wounded. I used my means to help the Americans. I have been told that the Government at Washington might think me worthy of a pension for the little time I have left to live, if the matter was properly presented."

Deeply wrinkled, swarthy, vivacious, the senora makes a striking picture in her scrupulously clean little home. American San Antonio has great respect for her. A portrait of her hangs in a place of honor at the City Hall. The State of Texas has acknowledged formally the part she took at the Alamo. Col. Tip Ford, the pioneer and old Indian fighter, believes the senora's story. There are some skeptics, and one of them is Tom Rife, the grizzled custodian of the Alamo. Rife has been here fifty-one years. He came after the Alamo had fallen, but in time to do some fighting for Texas. He doesn't believe the senora was in the Alamo, but his argument is more dogmatic than conclusive.

"I have known Mme. Candelaria fifty-one years," said Rife, as he was showing the way through the old fort. "She says she is 107 years old. According to that she had children when she was 65 years old."

Rife stops and looks at the visitors with an air of that settles it.

"Don't you think the senora was in the Alamo when it fell ?"

"No, I don't," replies the veteran, with emphasis.

"Then you think the story of her nursing Bowie is fiction, do you?"

"It's a lie," replies the veteran, choosing the shorter and plainer words.

But notwithstanding the skepticism of Rife and of a few others, it is common belief that the senora is to-day the only survivor of the Alamo. The story she told, as given above, was translated with care by her grandson, who repeatedly questioned her that he might be accurate. It differs in some details from the accounts previously attributed to her, and it embraces some points that are new perhaps.

Rife argues that because in the early years the senora did not publicly claim to have been in the Alamo with the Americans her later declaration is impaired. This is not a fair argument. The same conditions which prompted her to assume a fictitious name in her intercourse with the Americans would prompt her to make no public mention of her services as nurse to Bowie in the early years. Long after the Alamo fell feeling between Americans and Mexicans was intensely bitter. "Remember the Alamo!" was the terrible cry with which the Texans nerved themselves to slaughter without mercy at San Jacinto and on other battle fields. In later times there have been sporadic demonstrations of this feeling. The ashes and bones of Travis, Crockett, Bowie and their associates were never recovered. A few years ago an attempt was made to find some relics of the dead and to do them honor. There was a tradition that after the burning of the bodies the bones had been scraped up and deposited under the chancel of a church. Some one went to the priest in charge and asked him if he knew whether the heroes of the Alamo had been thus cared for.

"Heroes of the Alamo!" was the scornful reply. "There were no 'heroes of the Alamo.' They were thieves and robbers. No, sir; their bones are not under the chancel of this church. If they were, I would pay to have them dug up and thrown into the street."

Little of this sentiment remains now. But the senora had good reason fifty-one years ago to hide her identity and hold her tongue about her participation in the last scenes within the Alamo. She remembers where the funeral pyre was built. A beautiful little park in which the China umbrella trees grow with rare luxuriance, is on the spot. The senora also remembers where a hole was dug into which all that was left of the 172 bodies, after the fire had burned down, was thrown in. And that burial place is where the magnificent new Federal building stands fronting the plaza and the little park. Perhaps after all there could be no more fitting uses made—a park in place of the pyre; that which stands for the embodiment of the Republic in stone and mortar, where the bones were buried.

The Alamo still stands. And it will stand. Time can not do what the cannon balls of Santa Anna failed to accomplish. The Alamo was nearly a hundred years old when the Mexicans began to bombard its massive walls on the 22d of February, 1836. The cannonading continued at intervals until the morning of the 6th of March, and then the assault was made. There was a roof on the church when the siege began, the senora says. That was destroyed. The pillars and the beginnings of the arches are seen to-day. In one wall is a great crack. In many places the battering effects of the shots can be seen, but the ruin will stand for centuries. The church was one of the Spanish missions established at San Antonio nearly 200 years ago. This massive masonry must have taken years of labor. In the carved front is a stone with the figure 1757, and that is supposed to be the date of final completion. The church is in the form of a cross. On one side, in the corner, with a high barred window is the room where Bowie lay on his cot. Further back a passage through solid masonry leads to an iron door and another little room, which may have been the sacristy. The blackened niche in one side shows where candles burned long before Tom Rife came to keep the key. This chamber is in masonry. Walls and roof are inclosed solidly, save where the heavy iron door gives entrance. There is no window. Here the Texans kept their ammunition and the Mexicans attempted in vain to reach it with their cannon balls. At the last supreme moment, when he believed all had fallen but himself, Evans tried to fire the powder. This was part of the desperate plan of Travis. It was the act of Samson pulling down the temple. Had Evans succeeded, his act would have crushed beneath the falling masonry more Mexicans than were killed by rifle ball and bowie-knife. But

WHERE BOWIE DIED.

the striking of the match was delayed a moment too long. At the door of the magazine, with match in hand, Evans was struck down. What a culmination that would have been to the defense of the Alamo!

A convent was part of the Alamo Mission. An acequia, or irrigating ditch, to supply water to the mission ran through the grounds. It furnished water to Travis and the little garrison. Why did not Santa Anna cut the ditch and deprive the Americans of its use during the siege? That is one of the questions that has puzzled those who have groped for the history of the Alamo defense. Senora Candelaria says that the Americans had the use of the water during the siege. The reason why the ditch was not cut, she says, is that the Indians at the mission would not suffer any interference with the water system. There were some rights of the native population which even the despot hesitated to infringe.

More than the old church was included in the defense. A strong wall of masonry inclosed a space nearly 200 feet long and 120 feet wide. The church was in the southwest corner of the rectangle and was the headquarters and the storehouse for the garrison. A passage led from the chancel of the church into the yard. Through this the priests were wont to come from their convent on one side of the yard into the church to perform their religious duties, and through this the Texans fell back into the church on the morning of the 6th of March, when they were no longer able to hold the whole of the rectangle. It was at the northeast corner of the inclosure, diagonally across the yard from the church, that Castillon's column gained the first lodgment on the wall. The Mexicans swarmed up the ladders at that point. They stood upon each other's shoulders. The first who came were shot through the heads. The next were clubbed down as often as they reached the top of the wall. But there was a time when the heads rose faster than the bullets flew and the blows fell. The Mexicans stood upon the corner of the wall, too numerous to be beaten back. Then the Texans retired through the little passage into the church, piled bags of sand as high as their necks and made the last stand. Even when the Mexicans forced the outer entrances to the church, there was no yielding. When all of the defenders were dead below, the handful of Texans left stood upon the tower and fired charge after charge from a little cannon. With the recklessness

MISSION CONCEPCION.

of men who have shaken hands with death these cannoneers shoved into the piece nails, bits of iron, anything which would carry and wound. The little band could not be dislodged from below, and at length the Mexicans covered the whole eleven with one of their cannon, fired at short range and swept them away. It is tradition based upon the versions told by Mexican soldiers that one man was found alive in the tower. He was driven into a corner. He held his dripping bowie-knife in his hand. Nine bodies of Mexicans lay at his feet. He parried their bayonets as they came at him singly and struck them down. Three or four faced him and made a simultaneous rush. Pierced through and through, this last of the defenders died. Which one of the 172 he was tradition does not tell.

Only of late has the idea of preserving this historical landmark occurred to Texas with effective force. For a dozen years the Alamo remained as it had fallen. The interior was half filled with the debris of the siege, with the ruins of the roof and with the masonry knocked off the walls by cannon balls. Then the United States took possession, cleared out the wreck, put on a wooden roof and used the church as a storehouse for quartermaster stores. Deep down in the debris were uncovered several skeletons with fur caps and buckskin trimmings. No one need to ask on which side the owners had fought. In the hasty gathering of the dead and the wholesale cremation these had been overlooked by the victorious Mexicans. For thirty years the Alamo was desecrated; first by the Federal and next by Confederate and then by Federal authority again. The historic place was devoted to the housing of hard-tack and bacon. Texas suddenly awoke. For $20,000 the title to the cradle of Texas liberty was acquired by the State. The preservation of the building is assured, but the quartermaster's "improvements" are still in place, and about the only change that has been made since the hard-tack and bacon were moved out has been the location of a small tin box which dingy lettering says is to "receive contributions for the erection of a monument to the defenders of the Alamo."

But the Alamo has other historical interest. Spain was a vigilant mother country 200 years ago. She wanted the earth. She had laid hold of the West Indies, of Central America, of Mexico. And then she sent her representatives to occupy Texas and claim all to the eastward as far as the Louisiana possessions of France. Spanish aggression always moved with the sword in one hand and the cross in the other. And the sword was oftener in the right hand than the cross was. At San Antonio, Spain, in 1715, established with troops a presidio and with priests a mission. Troops and priests traveled together. These missions were queer institutions. The troops brought in the Indians. The priests converted them. It mattered not whether the Indian was willing. His soul must be saved. He was locked up at night. His back was scourged. And when conversion was assured the Indian was set to work to build dams, to dig acequias, to make gardens and vineyards. He quarried the stone, mixed the mortar and reared the massive walls of the Alamo and of the four other missions which are the wonder of all strangers who visit San Antonio.

"You will observe," said Tom Rife, the Alamo custodian, "that the original windows of the church are high up in the walls, far above your head. That was because the priests took no chances with the Indians. They didn't want to be hit with a stray arrow while they were engaged in their devotions. And they located the windows so high that anything coming through would pass over their heads."

The priests converted the Indians and made slaves of them, but they were careful to build convents which were forts, as well as churches, which would stand for centuries.

In the case of one of the missions at San Antonio, the record shows that the building was not completed until twenty-one years after the foundation stone was laid. Many an Indian convert's life went out in the good cause before the work was done. Riding up the Aransas Pass Railroad from the south in the early evening the traveler sees a strange contrast just before reaching the outskirts of San Antonio. A great four-story building, modern in all senses, comes into view on the right, of the arches, the cutting of queer designs, the font set into the wall. The roof of the chapel is of stone with arches and a central dome. It is said the great court-yard, which was inclosed by a wall of masonry, was four acres in extent. Outside of the church are arches which are all that remain to show the cloisters and cells of the convent. When Santa Anna approached San Antonio he expected to find the Texans fortified in this Mission. He regarded it as better for defense than the Alamo. The Alamo and the Concepcion churches were

THE SENORA'S HOME.

every window ablaze with electric light. It is one of the charitable institutions which Texas has built on plans as liberal as her prairies. The asylum comes and goes. And on the left there appears, in the moonlight, rising out of the mesquite and in the midst of tangled vines and brush the double towers of the Mission Concepcion. Just behind the towers is the Moorish dome. Humanity's best at the end of the nineteenth century is exemplified in the asylum. Humanity's best as it existed 150 years ago was worked out in the Mission. The ruin is well preserved. It is even habitable. The chapel has been used in recent years for a service by a bishop who venerates the past. The time was when a court-yard with walls of masonry inclosed buildings for school and military purposes as well as the massive church. Now all has tumbled down except the church, and that is in the brush two miles from San Antonio. Twenty-one years was none too long for the poor Indians to complete this work with all almost precisely alike. The Alamo had the disadvantage of standing where other buildings enabled the attacking party to approach it. One of the sallies made by Travis and his men was for the purpose of tearing down some Mexican houses which gave cover to the enemy.

Two miles below the Mission Concepcion is the Mission San Jose. These thrifty padres divided the land and the waters of San Antonio very well. They made great gardens with their convert labor, and they built the missions far enough apart that there might be no clashing of interests. There was competition in mission building just as there is in church architecture to-day. At Mission Concepcion the artists with the brush spread themselves upon frescoes not yet entirely worn away, while at San Jose the mallet and chisel were used upon the stone in the most wonderful manner. On the front, in the doorways, over the windows, wherever it was possible to carve a figure, that was done. The Mission San Jose has a single tower, but it is 60 feet high. Hewn logs arranged to make a circular stairway lead up to the second part of the tower. Thence to the lookout the ascent is by notched trunks of trees. The great stone roof over the main chapel held in place until a few years ago and went down with a mighty crash. One of the main walls has fallen. San Jose is a ruin, truly. And little wonder. Nearly a hundred years ago the priests concluded that missions which

THE PORTAL OF MISSION SAN JOSE.

enforced religion were a failure. The Indian converts had dwindled away. At San Jose there were not enough left to do the housework for the priests, let alone mind the ditches, the gardens, the vineyard and the church. When the lands of the Mission Concepcion were ordered partitioned to the remnant of the community which had been established there, only thirty-eight Indians—sixteen of them men, the rest women and children—could be found to inherit the property. The Missions taught the wonderful fertility of the soil, and showed to the white men who came after what could be done by irrigation. They furnished the Alamo and the Alamo made Texas. But as religious institutions the Missions were failures.

A MISSION INDIAN FAMILY.

It is history that the artist Huica came all of the way from Spain to do the finest of chiseling on the San Jose portal and windows. The work occupied him several years. Originally there were six life-size statues about the doorway, which is 35 feet high. Some of them have been carried off by vandals.

About two miles below San Jose is the Mission of San Juan. It is very plain, having neither the frescoing of Concepcion nor the elaborate carving of San Jose. On one side the very wide wall rises high above what was the roof, and has places for bells. Evidently the San Juan fathers had different ideas from those who controlled the other Missions. They put more work upon the granaries; upon the convent or monastery, which they made their home, and these are in a better state of preservation. That the priests at San Juan intended to build a finer church, is shown by the foundation walls of a chapel begun but never finished. The failure of the Mission system came before the plans were carried out. It has been said that these Indians who were brought in by the troops and turned out to the Missions to be converted became slaves. Perhaps that is incorrect. It is true that they were scourged for their shortcomings. At night the young men were locked in rooms on one side of the great court, while the young women were safely disposed of on the other side of the square. All arose at a given time. They had their allotted tasks. They attended to their religious duties. In short, they lived such lives as the priests thought best for their souls. But in a way they acquired community rights, and when the Missions went down the lands were divided among those converts who remained faithful and whose constitutions had been strong enough to stand the regimen.

In passing from one Mission to the next it is necessary each time to cross the river. The priests located the Missions on alternate sides. The Mission Espada—that was a well-chosen name—is below San Juan and on the opposite side of the river. When the visitor reaches Espada he is nine miles from the city of San Antonio. The story is that the tower of this Mission, carrying out the idea of the name, was in the form of the hilt of a sword. Mission Espada has been restored. Out of the ruins of the convent has been constructed a parochial residence. So much of the chapel has been rebuilt that it has lost its interest as a ruin. The walls of the great court still show how well prepared these communities were for defense against any foe without. At one angle is a round tower. It has indressed stone portholes for cannon, and above are openings for musket use. Loopholes were pierced in the walls at frequent intervals. There was need of such provision, for the Apaches often resented the presence of these communities. Fifty miles to the northwestward of San An-

MISSION SAN JUAN.

tonio at the Pass of Bandera the tribe had its stronghold. From the mountains, the Apaches swept down upon the Missions again and again. Sometimes they caught a few of the converts unawares. Occasionally they captured stock, but usually they found the watchman on duty in the church towers and the ramparts well manned by the whole effective force of the community.

The work of the priests reached high-water mark when the five Missions at San Antonio embraced 750 converts. After that it went down. Fifty years before Travis and his men occupied it, the Alamo had ceased to be a place for the reception and conversion of captured Indians. Convent and court had been turned into a barracks for troops. The church and its surroundings had come to be recognized as the military key to San Antonio. Around the Alamo, upon the plazas and along the streets there were many terrific contests and bloody scenes in the fifty years which preceded the battle of 1836. The followers of Philip Nolan, after their leader had been treacherously murdered by Spanish soldiers, were brought to San Antonio in 1800 and shut up in prison, into which part of the Alamo Mission had been turned.

OLD WINDOW, MISSION SAN JOSE.

From the Alamo marched forth the soldiers of Spain to hold back the Americans on the border. In 1811 the people passing the Alamo early in the morning saw between that and the main plaza a head on a pole. Col. Delgado, a flying revolutionist, had been captured and this was the warning to other would-be revolutionists. Gutierrez an associate of Delgado, escaped to the Louisiana border, joined a party of Americans led by Magee, an officer of the United States army, and came marching back. Americans, Mexican Republicans and Indians flocked to the standard and a small army appeared before San Antonio. The Spanish troops marched out from the Alamo to meet this motley crowd, and a thousand of them fell in the rout. The Governor of the province of Texas surrendered, and with him the Governor of New Leon and other distinguished officers. All were turned over to a son of the Delgado whose head had ornamented the pole in front of the Alamo. The younger Delgado started with the prisoners, ostensibly to go to the Gulf and send them to New Orleans. A mile and a half out of San Antonio the prisoners were stripped and butchered with knives. After that there was anarchy in San Antonio. The Mexican Royalist Government sent an army of 3000, under Elisondo, to retake the Alamo and to suppress the Republican uprising. Elisondo captured the horses of the Americans and reached the suburbs of San Antonio before his movement was discovered. But in the night the Americans marched out on foot and charged the Mexican army at dawn. With the loss of 1000 killed, wounded and prisoners, Elisondo was put to flight.

Then a provisional Government was set up in San Antonio and some degree of law and order was established. Arredondo came with 4000 men to do what Elisondo had failed to accomplish. The Americans and the Mexican Republicans calling themselves "the Republican Army of the North," marched out from the Alamo and fell into much the same kind of a trap they had set for Elisondo. This time the Mexican Royalists were victorious. Eighty of the prisoners were seated by tens on a log over a great grave and shot so that the bodies fell in a heap. Arredondo marched into San Antonio and threw 700 citizens into the prison for their supposed Republican sympathies. Eighteen of the prisoners were suffocated in a single night. Five hundred women of San Antonio were shut up in a building and forced to turn twenty-five bushels of corn into tortillas for the Royalist army every day. Thus until 1820 did San Antonio reap the whirlwind, and the Alamo, as fortress and prison, grew in historical interest. That year came Moses Austin from Connecticut with a proposition to bring a colony of Americans. He died, and his son, Stephen F. Austin, took up the project. In spite of imprisonment and killing, Americans kept coming. In 1831 the Bowies were here and the two brothers, with nine associates, fought 184 Indians until they had killed and wounded eighty-four, losing but one of their own number and having three wounded. The next year appeared in San Antonio Sam Houston. Then the Americans organized. A thousand of them joined Austin. Other leaders had smaller followings. Without much generalship they gathered about San Antonio. Some were for attacking the Mexican General and his force which held the Alamo and the city. Others hesitated about open hostilities. Three hundred volunteered to "go with Ben Milam into San Antonio," and in they went. It took four days of fighting to reach the Alamo. From house to house the Mexicans fell back, and from house to house the Americans advanced. Street after street was taken, until at the end of the fourth day the Alamo was reached. The Mexican General surrendered and with his troops was allowed to march away on parole. This left San Antonio in possession of the Americans for a few months. And the next and greatest step toward Texan independence was the fight at the Alamo. The story of which, from the only survivor's lips, has been told. W. B. S.

THROUGH TEXAS.

The Great Cash Crop Which Means Many Dollars Per Capita.

A King's Good Points—Proper Limitations on Monarchy—The Dublin Idea of Home Rule—Casting the Horoscope—A Coming Five-Cent Basis.

Special Correspondence of the Globe-Democrat.

DUBLIN, TEX., September 8.—Two months ago Texas began to report "first bales." But Texas has much latitude. It is weeks after the beginning before the cotton picking is fairly under way. From Houston across to chimneys of the gin houses are smoking. Around the cotton yards the barbed wire has been tightened on the posts and the bales are accumulating. Gin whistles toot a shrill and cheerful salute as the trains go by. This is Southern Texas. Every railroad station is beginning to ship. The cotton platforms are already covered with the early consignments. Samplers are going about, plucking out great wads of the staple here and tucking it back there. The scales and the marking-pot are busy. Empty box cars are being strung along the sidings. The new crop is moving—not as it will a month later, but sufficiently strong to make the transportation companies feel the impetus.

Middle Texas shows some picking in the earlier fields, and the prudent planter is culling out the already ripened bottom bolls. The top crop is not yet ready. Around the gin houses groups of men are busy putting in bracing posts, supplying missing planks, fixing up the engines and overhauling the machinery. The season is close at hand for Middle Texas. Further north there is similar stir, not quite so advanced, however. On Red River the top cotton is yet in blossom, but everybody is getting ready. The master of transportation is out on the railroad. He is the first one to hop off and the last one to climb on the train. He holds hurried consultations with station agents, asks when Smith will begin to ship and whether Jones has given notice how soon he will want to load

AT THE COMPRESS IN WACO.

"Santone" by the Mission route the fields are white. Far down the rows the pickers are bending over big baskets. In snowy mounds, here and there, the seed cotton is heaped up, waiting for the wagon. Along the country roads go great loads to be "ginned." At every town and cross-roads settlement the cars. He looks over the cotton platforms, with which every railroad station in the cotton belt is equipped, sees that planks are in place and that supports are strong. Then he moves on to the next station, to repeat questions and observation and to make more entries in his note book.

What a stimulus it is! Everybody and everything in Texas feels it. Two million bales. A hundred million dollars! Cash, too! Cash, which begins to flow the moment the first picker steps into the field, and cash which keeps circulating as the seed cotton goes to the gin, as the bale goes to the merchant and the seed to the mill, and finally, as the staple and oil and meal find their way through the factor to the markets of the world.

"Raise less cotton and more corn," the economist cries. That is very good advice, to a limited extent. But corn may be 15c or it may be 50c a bushel. Cotton may drop to 6c or it may bring 8c. Corn may be hard to sell at any price. Cotton will always bring ready money, even in advance, when it can be seen in the boll. Cotton pays the taxes and buys the sugar and coffee. It means new dresses and—most fascinating of arguments to the Texan—it means more land.

Hope rises and falls in Texas with the cotton prospects. The temper of a whole State is strung high as the crop nears maturity. Each turn in the weather is studied anxiously for its effect on the plant. And when the new crop is assured the strain is relieved and the whole State is happy.

The Texas farmer has yet to discover how cheaply he can raise cotton and live. When the price was 9c he kicked and said it was bankruptcy. At 8c and 7c he proclaimed that he was being ruined, but kept on planting. This year's crop was put in on a strong probability that it would not command more than 6c. It will not be quite so large as last year's, which was phenomenal in both acreage and yield. But it will be large enough. That is apparent already. The acreage is somewhat smaller than last year, perhaps about 15 per cent less. That is the estimate of some of the largest cotton handlers in the State. But they all admit that the reduction is not what it ought to be to restore prices.

"You see," said Mr. Wolfsohn, of the Dallas

A COTTON YARD AT BROWNWOOD.

Board of Trade, "cotton is the cash crop. If a farmer has got twenty-five bales of cotton maturing he can get a loan on it at any time. It is the best collateral that there is. The merchant can go to the wholesale man and show he has liens on 200 bales of cotton and get anything he wants. Cotton is collateral while it is growing; it is cash when it is picked. And while this is so there isn't much use trying to persuade a man to raise less cotton. My impression is that most of the arguments used last spring to induce farmers to cut down their cotton acreage were wasted. I think the Texas cotton crop is nearly as large this year as last."

An old cotton buyer who had dropped into the Board of Trade by accident and had heard Mr. Wolfsohn, took up the conversation: "I have seen 50,000 bales of cotton handled in Dallas," he said. "I have handled 250 bales in a day myself. The trouble has been to make the Texas farmer understand that he musn't buy corn. I have seen the Texas farmer raise cotton and buy all of his corn at 18c a bushel one year and at $1 a bushel the next year. It seemed as if he couldn't learn anything. I said to one of the biggest cotton-raisers, 'Have you any idea how much Texas will pay to Kansas for corn this year?' He said, 'I suppose about $10,000.' I said, 'By Jupiter, $2,000,000 won't meet it.' And yet the average Texas farmer would go along living on turnip tops and half starving until he could make the cotton crop, get a bale ready for market, rush into town with it and buy some side meat. I said to my cotton-growing friend, 'Perhaps you know what Texas will pay to Kansas this year for hog meat?' He said 'mebbe as much as $50,000.' I said, ' Over $2,000,000; and yet you fellows go on raising all cotoats. The one-crop idea has given place to variety. Blooded stock has been added. The bunches of cattle in the pastures have short horns, straight backs and massive shoulders. Naturally one is not surprised to find backed up by such a country an all-around little city. Dublin, almost new except the name, has street cars, electric lights, paved thoroughfares and a general look of prosperity. Her banker is from Maine. Her Mayor is a one-armed Arkansas Confederate who came in by ox train. Her chief business man and capitalist is from Elgin, Ill. They all pull together and the whole city pulls with them. Dublin has compress and oil mill for her cotton and seed, a tannery for her hides, elevators and mills for small grain, and has just sent a delegation to Kansas to buy hogs by the car-load to eat

SHIPPING OUT COTTON FROM DUBLIN.

ton and no corn and meat.' Well, things have gradually changed. To-day the Texas farmer is better off than he has been for seventeen years, in spite of the low price of cotton.''

Southwest from Fort Worth there is interesting evidence of the change the old cotton-buyer speaks about. Spinning the web of railroads, with herself in the spider's point of vantage, "the Fort" discovered two or three years ago that there was no southwestern radius to her network. A beginning was made. The Havemeyers, or some other mysterious New York influence, backed the enterprise. And now there are 120 miles of road in operation, stretching over prairies, through cross-timbers, by mountain gaps, from Fort Worth toward the Rio Grande. Dublin is brought into prominence by this development. And all of the way down to Dublin can be seen the new kind of farming in Texas. Every farmer has a patch of cotton, but every farmer has with the cotton a patch of corn. Often the corn patch is larger than the cotton patch. Wheat fields alternate with her surplus corn crop. The point to all of this is that diversified farming and diversified industry is the making of a model city in Texas. Until Dublin struck her steam-engine gait she had a struggle for existence which would have knocked out the average Texas town site.

The old stage trail from Fort Worth to Fort Yuma bowed down to the south and ran through this part of Texas. Perhaps because of a rocky road one of the stations on the trail was given the name of Dublin. Off to the left of the old trail looms Comanche Peak. From the summit can be seen ten counties of Texas. When the first railroad was built through this region and the stages stopped running, an attempt was made to obliterate Dublin. Another town ten miles away was started, the usual sale of lots was held and a depot was located. Dublin hung on to her autonomy. The old stage station wore out, the new town site got two railroads instead of one, and has become a city which can give pointers in thrift and public spirit to half of the communities in Texas.

The Dublin object lesson has a close relationship to the problem of how cheaply cotton can be grown in Texas. It proves that 6-cent cotton is better when mixed with wheat, and oats, and corn, a few pigs and a bunch of good stock, than 9-cent cotton with all of the supplies to be shipped in and paid for out of the cotton receipts. This is what Dublin and the country around about have demonstrated.

As a rule Texas farmers do not figure much, except on politics and dominoes. They can tell you the Democratic, Republican and Populist vote by township, county or congressional district at the last election. They can work off the ivory doubles and singles with great facility on the round table in the back part of the store. But when it comes to a show-down on the number of pounds of cotton in their last year's crop, the exact amount of land in plant, and the record of the days of labor devoted to it, not one of them in a thousand can give anything definite. And so it is very difficult to get testimony on how cheaply cotton can be raised in Texas. Down on the Aransas Pass road last year one cotton-raiser did what every farmer ought to do. He kept books on his crop. He had seven acres in cotton besides his grain and other things. He kept a strict account on the cotton just to see what it actually cost him. The seven acres produced 2,000 pounds of lint cotton. He got 7¾c a pound in San Antonio, or $155. His book showed that the labor—from breaking of ground to marketing, the cost of seed and all other claims which could go into the expense account—amounted to just half what he received for the cotton. The man and his boy did all of the "tending." Their work was put in at a fair estimate. The actual cost of raising the cotton was 3¾c per pound. The profit, which embraced also interest on the land investment, was $19.32½ per bale, or about $11 per acre. And yet, almost with one voice, the farmers of Texas claim that anything less than 7c for cotton means actual loss. The experience of the Aransas Pass man may be exceptional.

SCENE AT WEATHERFORD.

It is possible that he hoed cotton more and played dominoes less than the average farmer. The actual cost of raising cotton may be a great deal more than 3¾c a pound. The farmers of Texas owe it to themselves to emulate the example of the Aransas Pass man to the extent of keeping a strict expense account on the cotton crop and solving the problem of cost. Then they will be able to grumble upon a definite basis. Politics is pastime. Agriculture is business.

Not one farmer in a hundred will admit it, but there is probably a profit in raising cotton in Texas at 5c a pound. This does not imply going to Kansas for bread and meat. It does imply honest labor and good management. An all-day ride on an August Saturday across Southern Texas, from Houston to

San Antonio, revealed a rather astonishing situation. The towns in the famous Brazos country, "the black belt," were full of colored people. Mules by the hundreds were hitched at the railings in front of the stores and fringed the fences. Under the oaks, with their beautiful Spanish moss drapery, were refreshment stands. The smell of barbecued meat was wafted through the car window. Colored folks, big and little, were scattered about in groups. ·They came down to the stations and filled the platforms, returning the looks of curiosity with interest.

"There must be a good deal of politics down here." was suggested to a fellow-passenger who seemed familiar with the locality.

In Galveston men live by cotton, but plant not, neither do they pick. These entertain an interesting theory about the future of the king of crops. Texas, they say, now grows one-fourth of the cotton produced in the United States. Cotton is raised at less cost here than anywhere else in the country. The figures which represent actual cost of production in other States have no application here. And when the minimum at which other sections can grow is reached, Texas will have a margin of profit to her credit. Production may be reduced; it will be reduced, but not in Texas. The hill country of the older States will have to find a substitute crop or starve. Texas will go on heaping up the bales.

BRINGING COTTON INTO DUBLIN.

"Oh no," he said; "this is the regular thing. The niggers don't work on Saturday. They take that day to come to town and have a good time. Then they go to church on Sunday. You just watch the fields as you ride along, and you'll see there is nobody working in the black belt to-day."

It was so. The cotton was white. The empty baskets were scattered along at the ends of the rows. By the difference in color the line where the picking stopped the night before could be traced all of the way across the field. But in sixty miles there were not sixty pickers in sight.

If cotton gets down to 5c it may be necessary to work six days in the week. But at present prices there are no evidences that Texas is cotton-cursed. The latest returns at the office of the State Bureau of Agriculture in Austin show that, notwithstanding the depression, cotton throughout all Texas, well tilled and neglected, on good land and poor, yielded an average of $16.64 per acre. And that was $4 an acre better than the average of all other products.

She grows a fourth, more than a fourth, of the entire crop. Soon she will be making a third of this country's cotton. She has the land to raise the cotton crop of the world, and enough would be left to grow food for twenty-five times her present population. Thus the men to whom cotton means commissions theorize.

They do not look for any permanent return to higher prices. The tendency is downward, as it has been. Cheap prices last year may shorten the crop this year and stiffen figures a little. Next year or the year after, under the stimulus of better prices, there will be more cotton raised, and then prices will drop to a lower notch than ever. In the older States, these cotton men predict, there will be a fluctuation in the product following the fluctuation in prices. But the tendency will be toward lower prices everywhere and toward less acreage everywhere save in Texas. Here the production may not increase in times of depression, but it will not decrease. It may come to a standstill some years; then it will go forward. And gradually, after much seesawing, Texas will become the great cotton producing center of the world. In Texas the general tendency is toward increased production. Out of Texas the general inclination is toward decreased acreage. As for prices, the cotton men who dwell in the cities, with a few exceptions, expect to see 5c cotton without any panic. This, they say, is the logic of the situation. And, 99 out of 100 farmers to the contrary notwithstanding, the middleman holds that 5c cotton can't be grown with profit in Texas.

about overproduction, the amount in cotton was reduced a little. At least that is what the State Commissioner thinks. The amount of reduction, however, is not quite what the increase of last year was.

GINNING AT LEXINGTON.

It is a fact that in the face of steadily declining prices Texas has just as steadily added to her cotton product until this year. This is shown by the State Bureau of Agri-

PICKING COTTON NEAR CUERO.

culture. Five years ago the Texas cotton crop was raised upon 3,000,000 acres of land. Every year since then the farmers have added from 200,000 to 250,000 acres to the total. Two years ago the crop just turned the 4,000,000 acres. Last year the acreage took the usual jump and a little more. The increase was about 300,000 acres. This year, under the hue and cry raised early in the season

The land in Texas devoted to cotton is approaching 5,000,000 acres. It is claimed by the State bureau that there are within the limits of Texas 175,000,000 acres adapted to cotton culture. In the enormous proportions of the staple, transactions in a side product are sometimes lost sight of. It is the rapidly fluctuating industry of cotton-seed oil and meal. Last year was one of the good years in the cotton-seed business. Europe needed and took all of the cotton-seed meal and cake there was to sell, for stock feeding. At Waxahachie, an hour's ride southwest of Dallas, in the heart of "the black lands," the cotton-seed mill is said to have cleared 50 per cent on the investment. This year new mills are being built in Texas and old ones are being enlarged. The business may be overdone. But taking one year with another, the oil and meal and cake adds more than $30,000,000 to the value of the Texas cotton crop.

This Waxahachie to which reference is made above, is a wonder in its way. It is the largest cotton market for its population in the world. The little city has about 4,000 people. Last season it handled 32,000 bales of cotton, eight bales for each man, woman and child.

The time was when planters were bothered to know how to get rid of their seed. They let it accumulate in great heaps around the gin house until they were in the predicament of the Kansas farmer—he found it cheaper to move his barn than to haul off the manure. Now cotton-seed is worth all of the way from

$5 to $10 a ton, dependent upon the distance from the nearest mill. Agents for the mills travel through the State, gathering up all of the seed near enough to the railroad to pay for hauling. A ton of cotton-seed yields thirty-five gallons of oil. This oil goes in casks to the Mediterranean, and, in due course of time and trade, returns to the United States refined and in small bottles, with a foreign label which means "pure olive oil." Lard-packers use cotton-seed oil by the ton. The soap-makers sell it in the form of fine soap Lower grades go into tallow. The meal and the pressed cake are sent abroad to stimulate milk-giving in the English and European dairies. The hulls left from the grinding feed the furnaces of the mills, and the ashes from the hulls are bleached for lye. Cotton-raising as an industry has many sides to it. But from whatever point the view is taken, Texas has the best of the outlook.

W. B. S.

THROUGH TEXAS.

A Visit to the Largest Pecan Plantation in the World.

Mr. Swinden's Provision for Posterity—
The Natural Home of the Dessert Nut
—An Oil Boom that Collapsed—
Evolution Along the Concho.

Special Correspondence of the Globe-Democrat.

BROWNWOOD, TEX., September 14.—Away to the southwest of Fort Worth and Dallas, far beyond the Brazos, is a new kind of Texas. It has mountain peaks, great boiling springs day, in some part of Pennsylvania or Kentucky. He would never think of calling this Texas; there is no other part of Texas that resembles it. Two or three railroads have wandered out into this region and stopped. It took a good deal of coaxing to bring them. One town put up $25,000 and right-of-way as an inducement. The railroad built to that town and stopped. Then the next town raised $30,000 and more right-of-way. The railroad built to it. Thus, by alternate bidding and building, two railroads were "toled" out into this unknown country from 130 to 200 miles from their connections.

The largest pecan plantation in the world comes up to the suburbs of Brownwood. It is the ambition of every Texas city to have something that no other city possesses. Brownwood puts her best foot forward in a pecan orchard without a parallel. This is natural pecan country. From San Antonio northward through Brownwood and Santa Anna and Coleman and San Angelo, all of the way to Abilene, are groves of pecans. Every water-course has its fringe. When the first settlers came in there were twice as many pecans as there are now. But pecan wood is almost as good as its first cousin, the shellbark hickory. Before they discovered what a golden layer the goose was, the settlers had cut down the productive capacity of the pecan groves one-half. And now it is proposed to prohibit by legislative enactment the destruction of pecan trees.

A young man named Swinden came into the country. He didn't bring a dollar, but he had a good head. He got a place as clerk in a lumber yard and improved his opportunity.

A CONCHO COUNTY FARM.

of crystal water, pecan groves, 25,000-acre pastures and fertile valley farms. Dropping down into the midst of this region the traveler might imagine himself, on a bracing fall Seeing the growing profit in the harvest of pecans around Brownwood year after year, Mr. Swinden reasoned that if nature could do all this human intelligence could improve on it. Land in the vicinity of Brownwood was cheap. Swinden bought land and planted pecans. To-day he has 11,000 pecan trees growing. The trees are set out in regular orchard style. The land between the rows is cropped in cotton and grain. Very shrewdly Mr. Swinden has chosen the location of the orchard His trees are along the Pecan Creek, which has the finest natural pecan groves in this region. The house in which Mr. Swinden lives is on an elevation. Nearly the entire collection of 11,000 trees is in view from the window.

"when those trees are large enough to bear half a bushel to the tree, it will be something. Half a bushel to a tree means 5000 bushels for the orchard. Pecans now sell at $3 and $4 a bushel in Brownwood for shipping. It is not probable the price will be much less, for it takes a great deal of time and patience to grow pecans. When Mr. Swinden's orchard is yielding half a bushel to the tree the income from it will be from $15,000 to $20,000 a year."

The fame of the pecan orchard has gone abroad. Mr. Swinden receives letters of in-

ON THE CONCHO.

Pecans are of very slow growth. Those in the Swinden orchard are now a little thicker through than a good-sized thumb. The opinion of those who profess to know something of pecans is that it will take from fifteen to twenty years to grow a tree as large as a man's wrist. But Mr. Swinden is not discouraged. He is as heartily enthusiastic over the venture as he was when he set out the first tree. His plans comprehend more than the rearing of the trees. Looking forward to the time when the trees will bear, Mr. Swinden has already counted his chickens. There is a great deal of labor in picking up pecans one by one. In Mr. Swinden's orchard machinery will do it all. The pecans will fall when they are ripe. They will be taken up from the ground by sweeping machines very similar to those used on streets. Other machinery will clean. Then the nuts will be assorted according to size by still other machinery. Cleaned, culled and graded the Swinden pecans will be put on the market in condition to bring the top price. But when? Brooke Smith, the Brownwood banker and capitalist, says he doesn't believe Swinden's youngest child will live to see a full crop from that pecan orchard. "Still," said Mr. Smith,

quiry about it from all over the world. Some writers have evidently obtained the impression that the pecan trees are bearing and that the orchard is one of the get-rich-quick ideas. If it is, they want to go into the business, and they write for information how to do it. Mr. Swinden has not sold any pecans from his orchard. He has been able to eat all of the nuts that the 11,000 trees have produced thus far. He has not begun the manufacture of the gathering, cleaning and assorting machines, and will not do so at present. His first crop is in his mind's eye.

The growth is slow and the crop is far in the future, but the pecan is a great stayer. A pecan tree has never been known to die of old age. Brownwood people say that pecan trees live 1000 years. Perhaps they have counted the rings. Plenty of moisture seems to be a prime consideration of pecan growth. The natural pecan groves near Brownwood and San Angelo and all through this region hug the banks of the creeks fed by the living springs. They grow so close to the banks that their foliage shadows the water, and in the nutting season many bushels fall in. The pecan-growing business has reached the budding and grafting stage of development. There is a difference in pecan trees. Some trees bear larger nuts than others do. Some yield more regularly than others. It is the custom to improve the sprouts by grafting or budding from trees with the best records. There are pecans not much larger than a hazel nut. There are other pecans five times as large, with thin shells and well-filled meats, such as are exhibited in the rooms of the Brownwood Board of Trade by Prof. Carl Vincent.

selling all he could collect at 30c to 40c a gallon. The oil is dark olive-green in color. The discovery of its existence was made at a depth of 160 feet. The discoverer was satisfied with modest results. Other people were not. Companies were formed, and the country around Brownwood is dotted with derricks where drills have gone down as much as 1600 feet. But the findings have been disappointing. Oil is obtained almost anywhere within fifty miles of Brownwood, but it oozes slowly, just as it did and does in the original

GOAT RANCH NEAR SANTA ANNA.

The industry is well worth cultivating. Mr. Brooke Smith, the banker, considers the pecan crop a considerable item in Brownwood's prosperity. From the natural groves within the trading radius of this place the farmers bring in, when the season is favorable, sixty car loads of nuts. They receive $4 a bushel for them from the shippers. This little industry distributes $120,000 in cash in the region tributary to Brownwood. Half a dozen other centers, including San Antonio and Abilene, San Angelo and Santa Anna, Ballinger and Coleman, have their pecan trade. Brownwood's pecan crop is the equivalent of 4000 bales of cotton, which is about one-fourth of the amount of the staple which comes to this market.

A couple of years ago Brownwood had a great boom. The people thought they might resemble Pennsylvania in something more profitable than scenery. The idea got out that the pecan country was underlaid with beds of petroleum. Somebody in sinking a well had struck a flow which yielded from five to fifteen gallons a day. He scooped it up, found it was good, even in its natural state, and conducted a neat little business,

well. No "spouter" has been struck, and no great body has been tapped to encourage operations on a large scale. There was great excitement when the drills began to pound at

BORING FOR OIL AT BROWNWOOD.

Brownwood. Real estate went out of sight. It has returned within the limits of ordinary vision. Brownwood people no longer imagine they have another Oil City, Pa. They are not so proud as they were of the oily taste in many of their wells. They are trying to be content with the picking up of pecans, with the handling of 750,000 pounds of wool and 15,000 bales of cotton a year, and with the production of fifty bushels of red rust-proof oats to the acre.

From Fort Worth to Brownwood, 130 miles, is a region of farms of modern size and of diversified crops. Prosperous looking towns of from 2000 to 4000 people dot the way. Railroads intersect at convenient distances. Three colleges draw patronage and supply higher education. At Brownwood begin the big pastures. Beyond Brownwood the towns of any considerable size can be counted on the fingers of one hand. The railroads run just far enough to tap the cattle trade and come to dead ends. The big pastures are doomed. Public sentiment is strongly against them. That isn't all. The last train-load of cattle shipped from Brownwood this season netted the owner the beggarly sum of just $2.70 a head. A man who had a pasture of 17,000 acres cut it up into quarter sections and sold it out at auction. He had 500 men at the sale, and his land brought an average of $7.18 an acre. The big pasture men could stand off public sentiment some years, but the low price of cattle and the increasing demand for small farms is sweeping away the wire fences. Brooke Smith, the Brownwood banker, is the owner of one of these 20,000-acre pastures. He said in course of an interesting conversation on the disintegration: "I have had my land cut up into tracts of 160 acres, and it is for sale to small farmers. Any one who wants a quarter section can have his choice at $8 an acre."

The Overall pasture of 25,000 acres, owned and managed by a brother of John W. Overall, of St. Louis, joins the tract, 17,000 of which was sold so successfully at public auction. Col. Overall has declared his intention of cutting up his land into small farms and of selling to actual settlers.

SPRING NEAR SAN ANGELO.

The same idea has taken hold of other pasture men in this country on the Concho and the Colorado. There is fascination in the ownership of 15,000 to 25,000 acres of land all fenced. A man can get on the highest hill or peak in the center of such a tract and shout with all his might:

I am monarch of all I survey,

and the remotest echo will not answer back "you're a liar." It is hard to give up such a feeling. The pasture men have tried cattle and horses and sheep and Angora goats in the hope of finding profits that will keep pace with the increasing value of the land. It is of no use. A steer needs about twenty acres of land for twelve months' living. When that land is worth from $5 to $10 an acre the steer must go. So the pasture man will sell out to the farmer, move into the nearest little city, start a bank, collect interest on his mortgages and try to be satisfied with the new order of things. This is evolution in the Concho country. W. B. S.

THROUGH TEXAS.

Four Miles by Rail Out Upon the Gulf of Mexico.

A Ride on the World's Longest Jetty— Some Trade Experiments — The Wealth of the Oleander City— Fine Heads for Finance in the Forties.

Special Correspondence of the Globe-Democrat.

GALVESTON, TEX., September 26. — "In the first twenty-five days of June," said Mr. Gus. Reymershoffer, "we shipped out 22,000 bags of flour to Havana."

That was the real beginning of reciprocity for Galveston. The Reymershoffers are pioneering the way in new trade relations which concern greatly the whole Mississippi Valley. The experiments under reciprocity have gone far enough to warrant something more permanent. Galveston wants new steamship connections. She is negotiating now with a Philadelphia company to open regular communication with West Indian and Central American ports. Galveston also wants to get a line of two steamers which will start from here semi-monthly and reach the south as well as the north side of Cuba.

"Most assuredly we can get that trade when we get the connections," Mr. Reymershoffer said, raising his voice to compete with the machinery of the great mill. "That June shipment indicates to some extent what the trade will be. The consumption of flour in Cuba is enormous, and it can be supplied from Galveston. There was a Havana representative here a few days ago to make arrangements for shipments from Galveston. He went on to see the Fort Worth packery people, and then to Kansas, to open up a meat as well as flour trade by way of Galveston."

"Was this June exportation the beginning of your programme to rush up the flour trade between Galveston and the countries south of you, Mr. Reymershoffer?"

"Last year we shipped out from Galveston eight cargoes of flour. That was our pioneer year. The shipments were all made, however, from January to May. The experiment was fully encouraging. I have just had a report from our consignee at Porto Rico, in which he says that out of 1,900 bags sent him he has left only 650. We tried Rio Janeiro with a small consignment. The flour took well, but the trouble is we haven't regular connections. We need steamship lines. When we get the connections there will be no difficulty about taking and holding the trade."

"This Texas wheat is said to be specially adapted for flour in warm countries?"

THE GALVESTON BEACH.

"There is no doubt of it. Texas wheat is perfectly dry. Further north there is more moisture in the wheat. And the flour from the wheat with more moisture spoils sooner in a warm climate. As a matter of preference, we grind Texas wheat until the crop is all gone, and then we take Kansas wheat. The Texas wheat is a beautiful plump berry. It is richer in gluten than the California wheat. If we had not had an exceptional spring the wheat crop of Texas would have been immense. We prefer the Panhandle wheat to any other, if we can get it, because it is the driest and best."

Turning from the transaction of a matter of business with a clerk, the big miller of Texas took up, with added enthusiasm, the theme of wheat-growing in Northwest Texas.

"That," said he, "will be the greatest wheat belt in the United States. It will be greater than North Dakota. The region is larger, and all of it will be fine wheat country. We are getting very fine wheat over the Santa Fe from the Indian Nation and from Oklahoma. The conditions are much the same as in the Panhandle. The wheat is dry and peculiarly adapted to trade with countries south of us."

"That reminds me," said Secretary Brady, of the Galveston Board of Trade, who was sitting by, "that I have a letter from an Oklahoma wheat shipper who wants to form trade relations with us. He writes me: "There is a plow running over every 160 acres in this Territory wheat begins moving in June, and we ought to handle it right here. We have $18,000,000 capital here which ought to be in use the year round, and will be when our grain trade is developed."

"You have tried shipping out wheat, haven't you?"

"Yes," Mr. Reymershoffer replied, "I loaded the Alford, an English steamer, with wheat in ten days. It was an experiment. She arrived in ballast one day. The third day she came to the dock, and the morning of the fourth day I began loading her. In five days I put 55,000 bushels of wheat into her hold. She crossed the bar drawing 15 feet 3 inches. Three days were taken up with lightering. She carried 93,389 bushels. The experiment was entirely satisfactory."

"Have you tried corn?"

"Yes. People said corn couldn't be exported from Galveston. They said it would

THE JETTY, LOOKING TOWARD THE GALVESTON END.

Territory. Wheat is our staple. We are not satisfied with the treatment received in Chicago. Think we can do well by shipping to your port."

"The trouble with us here," said Mr. Brady, folding up the letter, "is that we have no grain board. There is no organization to which such a letter can be referred. What we want is a regular grain board, with a capital to' take business offered to us in this way. We have got elevator capacity of 1,500,000 bushels, and we have a mill here that grinds 800 barrels of flour a day. But grain business is new to us. You can talk to our business men and bankers about cotton, and they know all about that. But grain handling is a new thing. It will work in well with the cotton, when we get it started. The cotton season ends on the 1st of May. From that time until the next season opens on the 1st of September, our capital lies idle and nothing is doing. Texas and Indian spoil in transit. We formed a little syndicate just to show what could be done. We chartered the Propitious—pretty good name—and loaded 73,000 bushels of corn into her. We did it in May, the worst month of the year. The corn reached Liverpool in good condition, and we made our point. Just before we commenced buying for this experimental shipment corn was selling in Kansas for 14c. It was being burned for fuel. Our agents went into Kansas to buy. Before we got through the news of the intended exportation by way of Galveston got out, and corn went to 20c in Kansas. We didn't make any money, but we did what we started out to do—showed that corn could be shipped in good condition from Galveston. It was New Orleans which gave gulf shipments a bad name. We had another test here on the steamer Persis last November. She took out 104,000 bushels. She had an excessively rough voyage, and was out forty-five or sixty days, I've forgotten which. The report was circulated that she had been lost. But the corn reached Liverpool in good condition. There is no trouble on account of climate about grain shipments by way of Galveston. Railroads, of course, are interested in hauling the grain as far as they can. When we get deep water we will command the trade."

"When we get deep water," is what all Galveston is saying. And there is great impatience among owners of town lots because the outer end of the jetty doesn't creep faster toward the crest of the bar, which lies across the entrance to this grandest of American harbors. Uncle Sam builds slowly, but he builds exceedingly well. To a stranger it looks as if the engineers and contractor had made great progress. Of the long, narrow breakwater curving out and tapering until its line sinks into the sea, there has been finished 24,600 feet. A railroad track on trestle work is built above the huge work. The little engine which runs out over the track is more than half an hour making the trip from the shore to where the derricks are hoisting the five-ton blocks of granite and placing them on the wall. From the shore the engine and cars seem to be running on the water. Three or four miles distance wipes out the line of great rocks with the trestle above, and leaves only in view the surface of the Gulf and the train rolling merrily upon it.

fell below the five-ton minimum. They were rejected for outside work under the rule of the engineers, but will come in later for use where the breakers can not get at them with full force. The inspection is rigid. The shore end of the jetty was built up at a cost of $20 a

FIVE-TON BLOCKS AND THE MACHINE TO PLACE THEM.

foot. Where the Italian laborers are now lowering the granite blocks into place the cost is $80 a foot.

Galveston primarily, the Mississippi valley particularly, and the whole United States generally, are interested in this jetty building. Six millions of the people's money is going down into the depths in the hope that a deep-water channel may be secured for the exports and imports of the Southwest. The main jetty, extending out from the end of Galveston Island to the bar, will be 28,000 feet

A TRAIN-LOAD OF THE FIVE-TON BLOCKS.

Out where the jetty is being built now, the red granite is heaped up in large chunks. Nothing less than five tons is permitted on this part of the work. With anything smaller the waves, which sometimes roll in from 15 to 25 feet high, would play tricks. At the shore end of the jetty are scattered on the sandy waste several acres of rocks. These

long, perhaps a little longer. On the day that the visit was made with Mr. Hartrick, the United States Assistant Engineer, the report showed 24,600 feet completed. The granite blocks had been laid to 28,700 feet, and the apron of the jetty had reached 26,900.

"By October," said Mr. Hartrick, "we shall have this south jetty out to the crest of the bar."

After that there will be some anxious watching for results. The jetty is an experiment. Between the end of Galveston Island and the point of Bolivar Peninsula, Galveston Bay receives and empties with every tide. By cutting down that already narrow connection to one-half or less can the tide current between bay and gulf be increased enough to wear out a ship channel through the sand? That is the whole problem. When the south jetty reaches the crest of the bar the engineers hope to know more about the scouring possibilities. Some minor results have been accomplished. There is, or was, an inner bar. The single jetty has been sufficient to increase the scour over that inner bar. There was 9 feet of water on the inner bar before the jetty was built. There is 22 feet now.

The south jetty is only part of the plan. Heading out from Bolivar will be another jetty, not so long as the island jetty and not quite parallel, but gradually converging toward it. This will further cut down the channel, and increase the current and the scour. The place from which the north jetty is to start has been selected, and the work upon it will be under way by the time the end of the south jetty reaches the crest of the bar. Where the current is strong enough there is no difficulty in scouring out a channel. Thus, where the Bolivar and Galveston currents come together in the bay there is a depth of 80 feet of water. In a single year the current deposited 2 feet of sand alongside of the jetty. The only question is whether this confining of the water will throw the current to

THE GULF END OF THE JETTY.

Some prophets predicted that the current confined by the jetty would dig out a channel at the base of the mattresses and rocks and that some day a section of the costly work would cave and go down like an undermined bank on the Mississippi. But instead of that result the current has swept the surplus sand up against the jetty until there is a strip now in view where there was 14 feet of water. And on the outside of the jetty the sand is banking up in the same way. The end of Galveston Island on the Gulf side of the levee is growing and a thousand acres of land will be taken from the Gulf and added to the island by the jetty's deflection of former currents.

the right spot to dig out a channel. And will another bar, just as bad, form further out in the Gulf when the one against which the jetties are aimed is scoured through? These are things the engineers and the country will know more about when the $6,000,000 is spent. The play is for large stakes. The expenditures will be insignificant if the theory wins. And this will be the longest jetty system in the world.

Notwithstanding the impediment of the bar a great deal of trade comes in and goes out of Galveston with every tide. This is the richest city of its size on the continent. Possibly

Helena will dispute this. Perhaps it is better to say that millionaires are thicker on this Texas Island and in that Montana gulch than anywhere else, not excepting Manhattan. Interior Texas has sometimes kicked, holding to the theory that too many dollars have stuck to the fingers of the Galveston middlemen in passing through. It must be admitted that Galvestonians always were handy at the game of finance. As long ago as 1841 a scheme which would have made the eyes of a Populist dance was concocted on this strip of sand. The author was Gen. Mosely Baker. He proposed a bank. The basis was to be a loan of $5,000,000, which Gen. Baker thought could be got from France on an I. O. U. of the infant Texas Republic. The General intended to put the $5,000,000, when he got it, into the bank and issue paper money. He was going to put out $3 in paper for each dollar of this French credit. The paper money was to be loaned on notes for ninety days, with privilege of renewal for twelve months. Almost anything was good for collateral, but Gen. Baker expected to do his chief loaning on cotton in cultivation. Any cotton raiser could come into the bank and get this paper money to the value of half of the estimated yield of his field, the price of cotton being placed at 8c per pound. As security for the loan the cotton-raiser was to give a mortgage on his whole crop and also a mortgage on his land to double the amount borrowed. It is a great pity for this generation that this precedent of the sub-treasury idea did not have a fair trial in the '40s. Besides making money accessible to every man who had cotton growing, Gen. Baker was going to pay off the Texas Republic war debt with his paper. He expected that the revenue from interest on loans would pay all of the expenses of the Texas Government and relieve the people of both the tariff and direct taxation. Only one thing prevented the trial of Gen. Baker's scheme. France neglected to advance the $5,000,000 loan.

John Allen, of Mississippi, tells a story of an elegant Southern gentleman, unused to the ways of the world, who came to him one day, and with profuse apologies that he knew nothing about such matters, and with some stammering asked: "Ah, Mr. Allen, can you tell me how a gentleman should go about getting a little loan—a few hundred dollars say—from the bank?" "Certainly, Colonel," said Mr. Allen, "I am only too happy to be at your service. It is quite an easy matter. All you have to do is to go to the bank and sign a note and give your collateral. The bank hands the money over to you."

The old gentleman thanked Mr. Allen most earnestly. He said he understood it now perfectly, and felt much ashamed that he should be so ignorant in business affairs. He went away.

"About half an hour afterward I met the Colonel again," said Mr. Allen. "He came up to me with a pained expression on his countenance, and he asked, 'Ah, Mr. Allen, can you tell me where I can get that collateral?'"

Galveston has managed to acquire great wealth. This is made apparent in a collection of finer public buildings than is possessed by any other American city. The school buildings on Galveston Island cost

THE SHORE END OF THE JETTY.

more than all of the school buildings of Texas outside of the cities and towns. One millionaire's monument is a hospital, another's a chapel, a third's a high school, a fourth's the costliest private residence in Texas, if not in the whole Southwest, representing an expenditure of over $200,000. For private entertainment it is doubtful if any city in this country can show the equal of the Garten Verein with its spacious grounds, handsome buildings and lavish appointments. This institution is maintained by a club of Galveston's men of means. The beach is everybody's. All Texas lives from year to year on the memory of a plunge in a surf which does not chill the thinnest blood.

W. B. S.

THROUGH TEXAS.

Strange Sights and Discoveries of a Journey in the Gulf Country.

The Deep Water Triangle and the Possibilities Which Cluster About It.

A Round-Up of Turtles—Balcones Ranch —The Tomb of Dr. Bayard—How Five Dollars Built 600 Miles of Railroad.

Special Correspondence of the Globe-Democrat.

IN SOUTH TEXAS, October 19.—A strip of the native prairie 25 feet wide, a ribbon of turned sod 6 feet wide, and down the center of the ribbon, straight as the needle points, a row of pear trees. This, repeated thousands of times, is before the eyes of the traveler riding from Houston to Galveston. It is only two hours from the Magnolia City to the Oleander City. Much of the distance is over a coast prairie, 50 feet above the level of bayou and bay. From the car window the prairie seems to be perfectly flat, but there are slight grades, enough for surface drainage. A few years ago this journey was through a great pasture. As far as the vision reached cattle grazed. And that was supposed to be all that the great prairie, its sandy loam and its sub-irrigation, with inexhaustible water a dozen feet below the turf, was good for. Then a man named Stringfellow came down from the North. He wandered around over the prairie, poked holes in the sod, rubbed the loam contemplatively between his fingers, and said he thought pear trees would grow there. The few people who lived on the prairie laughed at him and said they had never heard of such a thing. Mr. Stringfellow said he would try a couple of thousand trees anyway. Then the natives looked serious and talked as if a man ought to be restrained from throwing money away in that fashion.

Mr. Stringfellow went ahead. He bought the land at $5 or $6 an acre, and could have got thousands of acres for the asking at that figure. He put in his 2000 pear trees of the Le Conte and Keiffer varieties. It has been about eight years since the ex-

THE FIRST HOTEL AT VELASCO.

periment was begun. These pear trees bore three, then five, then eight, and now they have reached ten bushels to the tree. A hole is dug in the ribbon of turned sod, just large enough to take in the year old roots. The soil is well packed around the roots. On the surface is strewn three good handfuls of cotton-seed meal. That is all. The little ribbon of turned sod between the strips of unbroken prairie is kept clean of weeds. Soil and climate do the rest. Pear trees flourish as they do nowhere else under the stars and stripes. A jury of his neighbors would have voted Mr. Stringfellow crazy six years ago. To-day he is the biggest man on all the coast prairie. He is Sir Oracle on fruit. His pear trees have revolutionized conditions. The $5 land is $50 land—a good deal of it. Thousands

THE SECOND HOTEL AT VELASCO.

of acres have been put into pears. And no wonder! Stringfellow's orchard was yielding $500 to the acre before it was six years old. People no longer refer to the prairie as the old salt marsh. Experiments in other directions than pear culture have been tried. One man has two acres in jessamine. He calls the flower the double jessamine. Last spring he sold $2000 worth from the two acres. As soon as the bud appears he cuts it with a stem 6 inches long. Ten buds and stems are tied in a bunch and wrapped in wet paper. One hundred bunches go in a box, and the box travels 1000 miles or more to some city in the still-frozen North, where the lovers of nature's sweetest odor quickly pay 15c, 20c and 25c a bud. The grower receives from $8 to $10 a thousand for the buds. It is a novel industry, but all sorts of unusual ways of making a living are being developed on the great prairie.

Next to the pears, Mr. Stringfellow, who is now abundantly honored as he was ridiculed when he came on the prairie, says the strawberry is the surest and most profitable crop.

He says this soil and climate will give $750 worth of strawberries to the acre. Picking begins the last of February, and by the middle of March the harvest is on. Real estate men, who still have some of the coast prairie to sell, say that five acres will support a family well; that a pear orchard five years old, as prices for the fruit now rule, and as trees now bear, is worth $1000 an acre. They say that the coast prairie can ship pears to New York as low as 37c a bushel and make a profit. The prices realized have been, up to this time, about $1 a bushel. It is one of the odd sights in Texas to see these pear trees shooting up so vigorously with raw prairie on both sides of the rows, and only the narrow ribbon of ground broken. Out in the

IN THE SUBURBS OF HOUSTON.

plain country, at Merkel, where everything luscious grows now by windmill irrigation, and where nothing grew except grass and long horns ten years ago, the horticulturists tell a story at the expense of the pioneer fruit raisers. They say that when the women began to get the idea that fruit could be produced around Merkel, they bored holes in the prairie with a post auger, thrust in an apple tree, rammed down on the roots three shovelfuls of fresh stable manure, and expected

AN OLD SOUTH TEXAS HOME.

to make cider the following year. This pear tree planting on the coast prairie approaches the Merkel experiment in labor-saving, but then, oh, what a difference in results!

Somewhere on the Texas coast there will be a deep-water harbor. Government millions may make it or private enterprise may find it. The experiment at the mouth of the Brazos River is interesting. A city was laid out there among the beautiful live oaks on the 1st of July, 1891. The first lot was sold ten days later. Within six months there was a population of 1,800 people. In July, '91, guests slept in a hotel made of timbers supported by a cross-piece. In July, '92, they stopped at a house which cost $75,000.

A corporation took hold of the mouth of the Brazos three years ago and ran jetties from both sides of it. The engineer was a man who had been associated with Capt. James B. Eads in the successful work at the mouth of the Mississippi. He planned a similar improvement. When private capital began to build these jetties there was a bar across the mouth of the Brazos and the water on it was only 4½ feet deep. In just one year from the time of beginning there was a channel of 10 feet in depth across the bar. In nine months more it was 13 feet, and at the end of the second year the depth was 15 feet. There is now between 17 and 18 feet of water, and steamships drawing from 14 to 16 feet go in and out of the mouth of the Brazos. This was done without a dollar of the Government's money. Velasco now claims that a steamship load of cotton has gone out of her port, drawing more water than any ship ever drew before in leaving a Texas port, without lightening. But Velasco wants 24 feet and more.

Houston, Velasco and Galveston are the points of a triangle, and within this triangle lies the old salt marsh, which has been turned into a great garden and orchard as the result of the Stringfellow experiment. It is forty miles from Galveston to Velasco across the bars of the triangle. It is fifty-five miles along one side of the triangle from Velasco to Houston. It is fifty miles along the other side of the triangle from Galveston to Houston. Developments and possibilities are near enough together here to be interesting and somewhat confusing. Somewhere within this triangle, or, perhaps, at one of the corners, or, it may be, along one of the sides, destiny will create a center of vast commercial importance. So the Gulf people firmly believe. When deep water, that is to say from 25 to 30 feet, is obtained, the exports and imports of 20,000,000 of people living between the Mississippi River and the Rocky Mountains will go by way of the Gulf of Mexico. "Through Texas" will take the place of "via New York" for a dozen Western States. This is the prize of trade for which Houston, Galveston, Velasco, Aransas Pass and the other places with harbor terminals on the Texas gulf coast are striving. The deep water will come. There is no doubt about that. The diversion of the foreign trade of the Mississippi Valley from east and west lines to north and south lines will follow. That is just as plain as the first proposition. But will the result be a concentration of the trade and all of its advantages at a single point on the Texas coast? Is that so certain? To one not interested in corner lots it looks as if there may be a scattering of benefits which will build up Houston, Galveston, Velasco, Aransas Pass and, perhaps, two or three other possible ports. It is very evident that the wise men of this generation have not been able to agree that one of these places, more than all of the others is the city of deepwater destiny. At Galveston they are pumping sand from the Gulf and making the long island grow in a way nature never thought of. When the jetties have done the work expected of them Galveston will have docks where the tarpon used to play. The creosote of the pile-treating works has not only stopped the ravages of the little toredo, but it has played the mischief with some of the great oyster beds of Galveston Bay. At Velasco they are planning for the time when steamships too long to turn around comfortably in the bosom of the Brazos shall come up to the docks, and they are preparing for basins and chutes which will facilitate the turning process. At an eligible looking place on Galveston Bay where the Dickson River empties, Chicago and Minneapolis capital has laid out the site of a brand-new city, sixteen miles from Galveston, thirty miles from Houston, and on the edge of the great coast prairie which is being cut up into orchards and gardens. Lumber is being delivered at the new site by the ship-load, and $1,500,000 will be spent by men who do not believe that Houston, Galveston and Velasco can take care of all the commercial advantages which are coming to the triangle. At another place on the bay the man who developed the whaleback idea in ocean tonnage is seeking a location for a great shipbuilding yard. Shipbuilding is one of the coming industries of the Gulf region. .It is accepted as a fact that ships must be built as nearly as possible in the temperature where they are to ply.

Houston keeps adding to her railroads until a round dozen of them center there. The farseeing real estate men have laid out heights and grand boulevards and parks for the homes of a hundred thousand people, of whose coming they entertain no skepticism. There is fascination about Houston for homes. When the landscape gardener comes he finds that nature has left little or nothing for him the city has lost its look of newness. Scattered through the residence portions of the city and out a little way in the country are the old-fashioned Southern mansions, with great columns supporting the roofs and the wide galleries. The war dealt gently with these relics in the Gulf region of Texas, and they stand to show what the South was, architecturally, before armies marched over it. Winding through the manufacturing district and among the railroad terminals of Houston is Buffalo Bayou. A deep, narrow river at the bottom of high and steep banks, it seems to be flowing at the bottom of a fissure. This is Houston's waterway to the Gulf. The bayou is no small part of the triangular situation. Its water is a curious deep reddish hue, but so pure that the boilers in the factories last far beyond the allotted time.

Houston is like no other Texas city. And it might be said that no Texas city is like any other Texas city. There is Fort Worth on a high plateau, with her proportions magnified

LOGGING IN THE PINERIES NEAR ORANGE.

to do but to lay out the drives and the walks. This is the magnolia city. The magnolia trees, 6 feet in diameter, are everywhere, and whether in foliage or in bloom they are wonderfully attractive to the stranger's eyes. The suburbs of Houston are natural parks, with pine trees towering towards the clouds, great wide spreading live oaks with the Spanish moss garbing their gnarled limbs and swaying in the breeze that blows from the Gulf less than fifty miles away. Houston has the old and settled look. Save in the additions which have sprung up under the impetus of this more recent growth, as by a mirage, until she looks like a second Chicago as seen five or ten miles away. And there is Dallas, nestled down by the Trinity and among the trees, without any revelation of her long business thoroughfares until the stranger is in the midst of them. Waco, with her seminaries and colleges almost as numerous as her hills, and cleanliness next to godliness in the form of a cluster of magnificent artesian wells scattered over billowy slopes rising and rolling back from the Brazos. Austin, the capital city, looks down from imposing heights reached by gradual ascent from the Colorado. And across the river there is another gradual ascent, on which loom up several of the State institutions, until the vision rises to a summit wooded and rugged almost as a mountain range. The capital of Texas is a city of magnificent views. And not the least interesting of her features is the great dam, thrown boldly across the channel and raised to a height of 50 feet, which suggests daring on the part of the engineer. This dam, it is said, has no parallel in the country. It is nearing completion and will have cost about $1,500,000. For this expenditure Austin obtains 16,500 horse-power. She will use the dam for her water works and her electric lights, and for other municipal purposes, and will have 14,000 horse-power to lease for manufacturing establishments. It is a bold scheme and illustrates the spirit with which Texas is awakening to her opportunities.

Without counterpart is San Antonio. And this is not wholly because of the large Mexican element which lives "over the San Pedro" and gives a foreign air to population, streets and architecture. A few miles above San Antonio, reached by a boulevard 100 feet of this strangest of rivers San Antonio is built. Within the limits of the city there must be two score or more of bridges over the river. In the days of early settlement everybody tried to have the river in his back yard, and this led to some queer surveying and street platting. Water for all household purposes was at the back door, and a bath house was a part of the equipment of every lot. On a Monday, the idler can lean over a San Antonio bridge and see the Mexican servants on both sides of the river, as far as the view extends, down by the river wrestling with the family wash.

South Texas is full of strange things. The strangeness is not the oddity of the freak. It is rather in the nature of surprises in products, in development, in industries, in scenery, in social conditions. In South Texas the traveler rides by rail thirty miles through one man's pasture. Within the limits of the pasture is a city and half a dozen settlements. In South Texas three distinct crops of grapes have been taken from the vines in twelve months. Two crops is the regular thing in the vineyards below San Antonio. The fruit-

BALCONES RANCH.

wide and paved from curb to curb, the river has its beginning in a collection of immense springs. Right out of the bosom of Mother Earth the water rises. The pools are 50 feet across. They are transparent to the bottom. Down in the depths of vegetable growth waves and bubbles are continually arising. These are the only indications of the inflow. But from the lowest rim of each pool there goes out a stream of water perhaps as large as a man's body, perhaps equal to the largest main in a city's water works. The stream joins with other streams, close at hand and the San Antonio River, biggest at its birth, starts on its way to the Gulf. It wriggles and curves until it almost returns to itself in a dozen places, and close up to the borders growing development of California and Florida has been heralded to the world. But the possibilities of the Texas Gulf region in that direction are only just beginning to be known to the people who have lived there all of their lives. From South Texas came a man who built 600 miles of railroad with a five-dollar bill and faith, and the bill was a borrowed one. He moved up from Corpus Christi to San Antonio with all of his possessions heaped on a two-wheeled cart. He got a charter to build a railroad from San Antonio to Aransas Pass. He graded a mile of it, throwing a good deal more than one shovel of dirt with his own hands. The receiver of another road loaned this indefatigable builder enough old rails for a mile of track. In a distant part of the State was purchased an engine which had been condemned six years before and sent to the shops to be wrecked for scrap-iron. Two old cars were picked up somewhere else at a bargain. And that old engine, drawing those old cars, steamed into San Antonio. On engine and cars in bold lettering was painted in lamp-black, "S. and A. P." With one mile of old-rail track and with the equipment of the old engine and the two old cars Uriah Lott started the Aransas Pass system. There has been some tall financiering in the history of railroad building in this country, but there isn't anything which, for dazzling pluck, quite approaches the story of the building of this 600 miles of road in South Texas. To the one mile of track three were added—three miles by a dicker for some second hand rails which a street car company had bought from a narrow-gauge company. On this basis a credit trade was made with a Pennsylvania rolling mill for ten miles of rails. When they arrived there wasn't money enough in the treasury to pay the freight, But it was got somehow. Ten miles of track gave the foundation for bonds which built forty miles more, and so the system grew into its present proportions. This man who built the Aransas Pass system rode from San Antonio to Chicago, at one critical period in his enterprise, without a cent in his pocket. He had transportation, but he hadn't anything to buy food, and he went through hungry.

The strangest thing at Aransas Pass is a certain live-stock industry. Behind the pass, upon what are called "the middle grounds," grows a peculiar kind of sea weed. It has its roots far under water. This weed is the favorite food of the green sea turtle. There are bull turtles and cow turtles and turtle calves. They come in herds from nobody knows where, to graze fathoms deep on the tender ends of this weed. They come and feed and go without ever showing themselves willingly on shore. The old idea of turtle hunting is to catch the unwieldy animal napping on the sand and flop him over on his back before he can wabble down to his native element. But that is not the kind of turtle catching pursued at Aransas Pass. Nets like those used for fish, only made of much stronger twine, are strung along in convenient places near the turtle pastures. They are attached to floats. The turtle catcher knows the hours at which the herds usually seek or leave the pastures. He leaves his camp on the beach and goes out in his boat to a convenient distance from the nets, and there he waits and watches for a violent agitation of the floats. The nets are not set with the idea that they will inclose the turtle. They are stretched out to cover as much space as possible with the expectation that, going to the pastures or coming from them the turtle will strike the net with his flippers and become entangled in the meshes. Early morning is the best time for catching. And the turtle is hoisted out of the tangle and into the boat as quickly as possible. There is no danger of the net being cut for the green sea turtle, unlike his snapping relative, has no teeth. But the species is very strong with the flippers, and may break some of the net if left to flounder around too long.

On his back in the bottom of the boat goes the monster, and there he is harmless and helpless. The state of captivity is completed by tying the flippers across the under shell. After that the catcher goes on looking for more. Unless the head is allowed to drop too far back the turtle will live comfortably a month or more on his back in the bottom of the boat. But it isn't usual to apply the test of endurance to such a degree. Once a week the turtle-catcher hoists sail and runs over the bay to the store houses. There are pens in shallow water made safe by heavy stockades of posts driven close together. In these

THE GREAT DAM AT AUSTIN.

pens the turtles are turned loose with about the same freedom that cattle are given in the yards at a shipping point. And they are as docile as cattle usually are when thus suddenly deprived of liberty.

Affliction's sons are brothers in distress—

in turtle as well as other kind. The turtles lie quietly in the pens, with only an occasional protest. Now and then some monster will rise to the surface, raise his head and bellow hoarsely. The sound is rather awe-inspiring, but really the only danger in handling the turtle is from a stroke of the flippers, and the kick is not very bad. It is no easy job, however, to lift them about. Some of the bull turtles run up to 650 pounds. That is as much as a yearling Texas steer will weigh. A good average weight is 400 pounds. The turtle calves weigh from 40 pounds upwards.

A VELASCO HARBOR SCENE.

The turtles selected for shipment go all of the way to New York and other epicurean centers alive. They are put into wooden frames called crates. There they lie on their backs with their heads propped up. The pillow is a very essential part of the preparation for the journey. A turtle's back breaks more easily than one would suppose, and then he is a no account turtle for a long journey. From thirty to fifty turtles go by a single shipment. They are sent to Galveston, and from there they travel by steamer. People who pay for green sea turtle soup at the rate of 5c a spoonful can figure out the profit in a 650-pounder. There is more profit in Texas turtles than in Texas steers. For four years Aransas Pass has been shipping turtles in large numbers, and the herds show no diminution.

For the disposition of those turtles which are not sent out alive there is a cannery on the island. Turtle canning is as interesting as turtle catching. Scrupulous cleanliness is the first rule. It even precedes the "first catch your turtle." The turtles are dressed and then all of the flesh is put into great cooking pots. This part of the process stops before the flesh is entirely cooked. It is continued just long enough to separate the divisions. There are sixteen kinds of meat in a turtle. Each kind has a distinct flavor, and at the cannery it is known by a separate name. It is called by what it most resembles. In a turtle are found chicken fat, pork fat, veal, mutton, beef meat, duck, and so on through the sixteen varieties. Partial cooking makes it possible to divide the varieties. When this has been completed, each variety is cut into small fragments. Experts take the cans and passing from heap to heap take from each the proportion which experience has shown to be about right for obtaining the true combination flavor. Into each can is dropped a contribution from each of the sixteen varieties. The contents of the can are brought to the boiling point and then the can is sealed and is ready to carry the material for genuine green sea turtle soup to any part of the world. With one of these cans and a pot any cook can turn out green sea turtle soup on short notice.

THE TOMB OF DR. BAYARD.

In no Northern cities and towns of corresponding population can such costly private residences be found as in Texas. Perhaps an exception should be made of the East, where millionaires retire to their early homes and build palaces. But where is there the city of 20,000 people in the Mississippi Valley with a private residence that cost $200,000. Texas can show a dozen homesteads which represent that investment. She has a hundred which cost half as much. As for the $75,000 and $50,000 mansions, they are to be found in all parts of the State.

The peculiar Texas homestead law is perhaps largely responsible for this. In his flush period the merchant, the ranchman, the speculator socks his cash into the brick and mortar of a home, and he knows it will stay there. No execution can reach the homestead, even if it cost a million, so long as the taxes are paid. A Texas homestead is $5000 worth of land in city or town, or 200 acres of land in country, with all the improvements there can be upon it. Once paid for it can not be taken away for any debt or business misfortune that may come upon the owner. To the Texan who wishes to lay by for a rainy day or for heirs the homestead is safer than life insurance. It is his castle. The law's porticullis falls in the face of the creditor. If the homestead be a farm, the growing crops share the exemption. If upon his $5000 worth of city property, the Texan chooses to build a business block at the cost of $100,000 or more and call one room in it his dwelling place he can bid defiance to all bills and judgments. The law is occasionally abused, like most other laws. There have been unscrupulous men who put not only

PICKING GRAPES IN THE COAST COUNTRY.

their own, but other people's money into a Texas homestead and then "failed." But the general tendency of the law is to encourage the building of homes, and fine homes, too. "Here is something that can't get away," the home builder says, and he puts in the money with a free hand. The result is this unusual array of costly mansions in all of the Texas cities.

The exemption law of Texas has many provisions. It is almost a blanket. Besides the home, all furniture and provisions are beyond the reach of the creditor. Implements and tools and books cannot be touched. And in addition to these the resident of Texas can hold, against execution, five cows and their calves, and two yoke of oxen, one gun, two horses and a wagon, a carriage or buggy, all saddles and harness necessary for family use, twenty head of hogs and twenty head of sheep and the current wages. This is a curious law. The men who sell sugar and flour, meat and potatoes, clothes and shoes and other things sometimes grumble because they can't collect their bills. But then, on the other hand, this is a great State for the poor man. It is easier to accumulate in Texas than anywhere else in the Union. Even the Texas tax-gatherer has a thus-far-and-no-farther line drawn across his pathway. Death and taxes may be the sure things everywhere else, but in this State taxes stop short of something. Farm products in the hands of the farmer and family supplies for home and farm use are not taxable. The sewing machine is beyond the reach of the collector, and with it $250 worth of furniture. The laws of exemption from execution and from taxation are very favorable to the agriculturalist, more so than anywhere else in the South or North. This may explain why only 9 per cent of the population of Texas is found in cities, while in Illinois the urban proportion is 53 per cent, and in other States from 40 to 50 per cent.

There is another class of queer things in Texas. At Boerne the people show the visitor the strange conceit of the late Dr. Bayard. It was so many years ago the Doctor came to Texas that nobody can tell just the date. He was eccentric as long as the neighborhood chronicles reach back. By the occasional practice of medicine, by tilling a little farm and in various ways the Doctor made an easy living and had much leisure. In his spare hours he chiseled out a tomb for himself in the rock. In the first place he dug a shaft, almost perpendicular. On top he placed a door. A ladder let him down as the work proceeded. At what he conceived to be a convenient depth, this eccentric character slowly and laboriously hewed out in the solid rock a niche in which he could lie comfortably. For several years before he died he was in the habit of going down into the tomb, stretching himself out and waiting for the summons. Death did not accede to the hermit's wishes. It came like a thief in the night. Neighbors carefully carried out the instructions left. They took the body down the ladder, put it in the niche and cemented the cover. Dr. Bayard, in an unusual fit of confidence, told that he was one of the Bayards, of Delaware, but he never explained his self-imposed exile or accounted for his peculiar ways.

In Southwest Texas is the famous Balcones ranch. It is a monument to a class who helped to give Texas her peculiar reputation. Balcones ranch was "improved" by a wealthy Englishman who came out from the old country with a pocketful of money and his head full of ideas of a good time. He put on the raw land the usual improvements, and then he added a race track, a polo ground and various diverting institutions. While the money lasted and "Me Lud" lived the fun was fast and furious for everybody who chose to come. But the end of a check book and of a fast life were reached together. Balcones ranch is now conducted on more sober lines for what there is in it.

Orange, on the Sabine, is where the saw mills are eating up the pine logs at a rate which would exhaust a supply less magnificent than Southeast Texas furnishes. On the principal street in Orange stands a massive oak tree. Until a few days ago there projected straight out from the tree over the street a strong limb about ten feet from the ground. On one side of the Sabine is Texas and on the other Louisiana. The lawless element for many years found it easy to cross from one side of the Sabine to the other and dodge the consequences of crime until the indignation of the public mind had subsided. Twice Orange lost a Sheriff at the murderous hands of this element. And twice the murderer was brought in and swung off from that oaken limb so conveniently overhanging the chief thoroughfare of the city. On one or two other occasions nature's gallows has borne fruit. But the limb has gone. A man with a saw climbed the oak tree and in ten minutes the limb fell, while the city looked on approvingly at the unspoken suggestion that hereafter the law be allowed to take its course.

When Sam Bass, the famous stage and train robber, died, his body was buri d at the cemetery at Round Rock. One morning the community arose to find that a neat monument had been placed at the head of the grave by unknown hands in the night. The inscription was, "Here lies a brave man. Why was he not true?"

This class of queer things—the oaken limb at Orange, the hurrah life at Balcones, the career of Sam Bass and his imitators, the Dr. Bayards—is mentioned to point the assertion that it belongs to the past of Texas. It gave the State a reputation for eccentricity and for general wild-and-woolluness. That reputation is not sustained by what can be seen now in a trip "Through Texas." W. B. S.

THROUGH TEXAS.

A Look Backward, from the Exit, at the Great Commonwealth.

Gov. Hogg Coming North—For Capital and Immigration, "By Gatline!"—Some Facts by Way of Comparison—Mr. Exall as a Seer.

Special Correspondence of the Globe-Democrat.

TEXARKANA, TEX., October 28.—"Through Texas!" It means much. Due west across the State from this eastern edge to El Paso on the Rio Grande, straight as the crow flies, is a longer ride than from St. Louis to New York. If one travels over all of the railways within the borders of Texas he will pay $558.66 in fares. So a railroad man with a head for statistical information figures. But it is possible to get some idea of the immensity of the State at less expense. Any one can take a map of the United States and fold it. Try the experiment lengthwise first. The northern boundary of the Texas Panhandle will follow closely the middle crease, and the southernmost point of Texas will lap far over North Dakota into the British Dominions. More than half of our latitude is embraced within the north and south line of Texas. Now fold the north way with Texarkana in the crease. El Paso's opposite is out in the Atlantic Ocean far east of Savannah and the line of Georgia. Fold again on El Paso as the axis. Texarkana lies in the Pacific Ocean beyond San Diego. "Through Texas" is more than one-third of the way across the continent from Charleston, S. C., to Los Angeles, Cal.

Take the map again and clip out all of New England. It drops upon the Panhandle of Texas and nowhere touches the border. Add to all of New England all the so-called Empire State of New York, the Keystone State of the Union, Pennsylvania, that foreign power, New Jersey, little Delaware, Maryland, My Maryland, and the Old Dominion, Mother of Presidents, Virginia. Now the broad domain of Texas begins to disappear.

Just out of Dallas Mr. Henry Exall has what many consider the model farm of Texas. He, however, says he cultivates only "fairly." The farm embraces 500 acres. This year Mr. Exall had 100 acres of wheat, 100 acres of oats, 100 acres of corn and 200 acres of grass.

"My wheat," said Mr. Exall, "yielded thirty bushels to the acre and my oats sixty bushels. That is actual machine measure, not estimate. The corn will go at least sixty bushels. It stands two stalks in a hill with the ears turned down. I don't know that these crops can be attributed to an unusual season. We have had favorable weather; but it is a fact, I think, that there is no country in the whole universe which has the equal of this black land. The soil is of peculiar formation. It is the combination, in just the right proportions, of decaying vegetation and disintegrating limestone. We have land here which has been in cultivation every year for twenty-five years, and without a pound of fertilizer. It produces just the same now as it did at first. It seems to have the inherent quality of entire recuperation without any outside help. Our land averages 41 per cent of a bale of cotton, and there isn't $5 paid for fertilizer in the whole State. In the cotton-growing States outside of Texas, the average is 38 per cent of a bale with all of the hundreds of thousands of tons of fertilizer."

"How much can you make on cotton at present prices, Mr. Exall?"

"I don't raise any cotton. I have land besides my Dallas place, in other parts of the country, rented on shares. In wheat and oats this land pays me over $7 an acre for my share of the crop."

"For what can such land be bought in Texas?"

"The same character of land a little further from town can be got for from $10 to $25 an acre. Near town the prices are higher. But let me tell you our land is held at only one-fourth the price of land similarly situated in the North. Land in Illinois, for instance, held at $40 an acre can be bought in Texas for $10 an acre. This $10 land will produce as much as the $40 land in Illinois. Here we have the advantage of mild winters. It takes less to care for stock. Food is fuel, you know. If you don't have to supply the fuel the material goes into growth and flesh!"

"There is money in thirty-bushel wheat even at low prices, isn't there?"

"I don't grow wheat for wheat. My object in sowing is to have grazing for my horses. I pasture them all winter on the wheat and take them off in February. My purpose is to show as high-classed horses bred here in Texas as can be exhibited anywhere in the Union. Not only that, but I want to show the people here that the period of most profitable growth is youth. I have yearling colts and not sixteen months old which are 15½ hands high. This is not because there is any thing extraordinary in the colt, but because he has had what he needed. I don't believe it is well for a colt to starve to make him tough. Nor is it the thing to raise stock on climate, as some farmers do. The idea in Texas has been to apportion to the animal so much grass for the year and then exercise no discretion as to how the feed shall be distributed through the period. We have got the limestone for which Kentucky claims so much, and we've got milder winters, so that we can have our colts come when we please and keep them growing all the time."

Mr. Exall is the owner of Electricite, bred by Senator Stanford and the highest-priced horse in Texas. He has great hopes of developing a famous trotting strain that shall be peculiarly Texan.

"I wouldn't exchange him for any other horse that lives," he said. "I have no price put upon him, but I wouldn't take $100,000 for him. For a long time I have known that the toughest horses were these Texans, but we didn't get very good results. The reason was that we didn't have the proper pedigree. I believe now we've got it. Electricite is one of the best bred colts ever foaled. His sire was Electioneer, the greatest progenitor of trotting stock."

Mr. Exall is not a Texan by birth; he is a Virginian, but, like a good many other Texans by adoption, he is more intensely loyal than the average native.

"When this country of ours had 30,000,000 of people where were they?" asked Mr. Exall. "East of the Mississippi, weren't they? And when the population had swelled to 60,000,000 what had happened west of the Mississippi? When we have 100,000,000 people, where will they live? Have you ever thought of that? When the population of the country went up from 30,000,000 to 60,000,000, the whole region west of the Mississippi was open to receive them. Now, when our population is to go from 60,000,000 to 100,000,000, the only productive land that is open is in Texas. The line of settlement, without irrigation, has been pushed about to the limit in the West and Northwest. Texas alone presents any great amount of unoccupied land. You may think I am something of a crank on this subject, but I only ask you to look at what has happened in the last thirty years. Immigration is still pouring in and the country is growing faster than ever. People have got to live somewhere. Texas cities are too small instead of too large. In Illinois 55 per cent of the population is in towns of over 10,000 population. Texas has 9 per cent of her population in towns of over 10,000. The city of Dallas, with 50,000 people, has 1,500,000 people within 125 miles. No such condition exists in America, where there isn't a city two or three times as large as Dallas. Yet we are the largest city within 500 miles of us in any direction. With such a country, such products and such opportunities for immigration there should be a city of 200,000 people. We shall wake up here some day and find that we haven't the commercial center to meet the demands of trade around us. I tell these people they don't realize what the conditions will be in Texas in ten or fifteen years."

When people live as thickly in Texas as they do in Illinois, this State will have 14,000,000 population. With as many people to the square mile as New York State has to-day, Texas could show a population of 27,600,000. With the same number in proportion to area that New Jersey counts Texas would be supporting 63,800,000, or more than all counted in the last census for the whole United States.

There will have to be some mighty changes down here before Texas realizes on her possibilities. In Dallas the sales of agricultural implements amount to $12,000,000 annually. No other city in the United States makes such a showing.

Henry Exall said to John Deere, the plow maker, not long ago, "Why don't you manufacture implements in Texas for Texas trade?"

"It isn't any use," said Mr. Deere. "You people will buy and pay for the cost of transportation."

"Well," said Mr. Exall, "we are going to manufacture implements in Texas."

"That's different," commented Mr. Deere. "Then we'll come to Texas and manufacture, too."

Texas has everything in natural resources. It is only a matter of development. Metal and wood working in all branches will have to come. That there should be a haul of hundreds of miles between the manufacturer and the millions of Texas consumers is not in the nature of things, with such forests and such ore deposits as there are here. To-day there is a string of cotton factories from Denison, on the north line of the State, to Galveston, on the Gulf. This is only a beginning. Texas will not only raise her own wheat, save her bacon and make her clothes, but she wil manufacture her own implements and vehicles, and roll her own steel rails, which will make her first instead of third or fourth among the States in mileage. It is in the direction of varied industry that the future greatness of Texas lies.

"We want young blood and more money in Texas. I believe I can assist in getting both. As soon as my duties will admit, I am going North to mingle with the people and tell them what we've got for them in Texas." So said Gov. Hogg a few days ago.

"Yes, sir," he added, "in a few months, when I shall have entered upon my second term, I am going to make a trip through the North, and, by gatlins, I am going to say to the people up there that their sons and daughters will be as safe in Texas as they are while walking the streets of Boston."

.W. B. S.

www.ingramcontent.com/pod-product-compliance
Lightning Source LLC
Chambersburg PA
CBHW020149170426
43199CB00010B/949